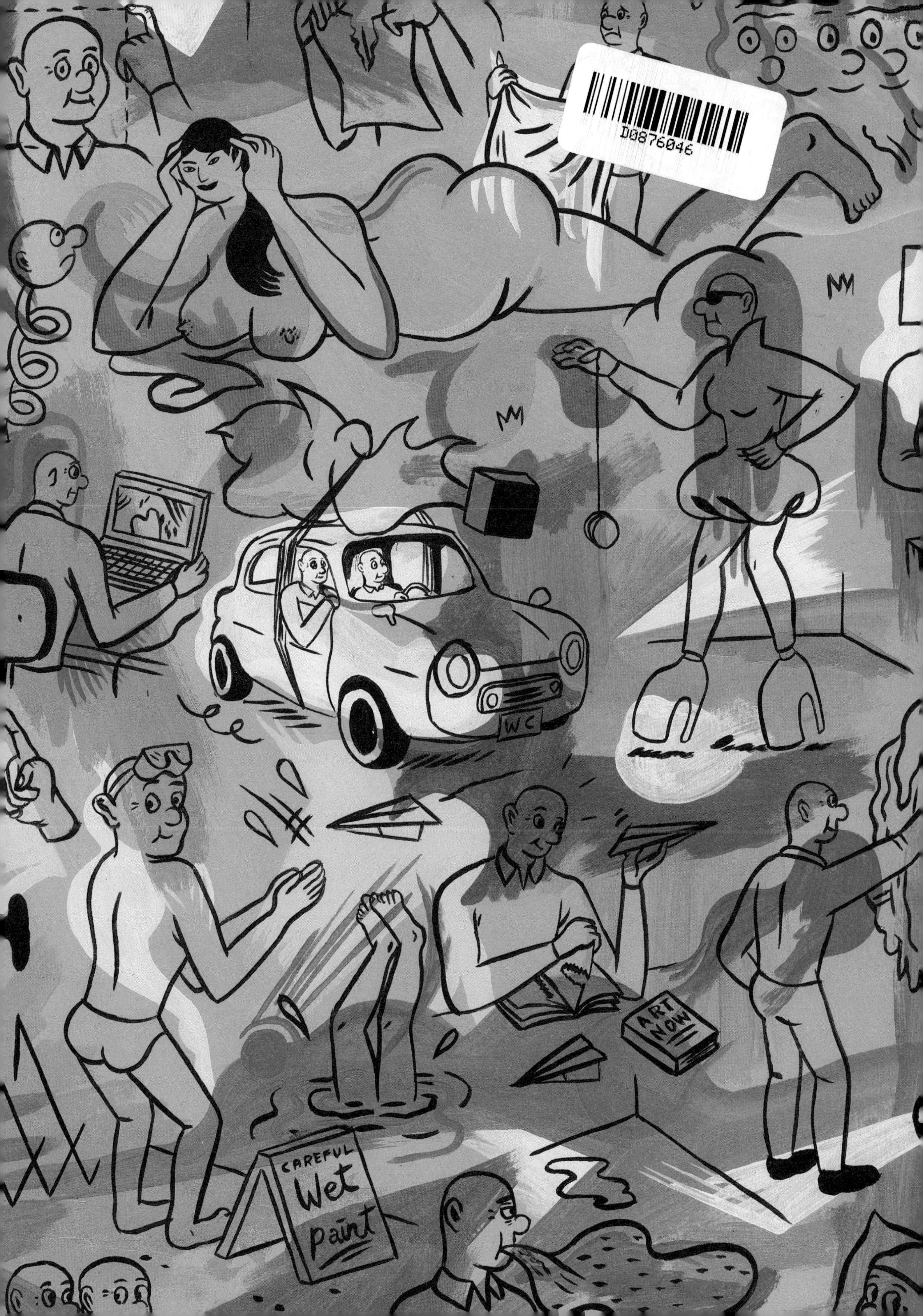
WC
ART NOW
CAREFUL
Wet
paint

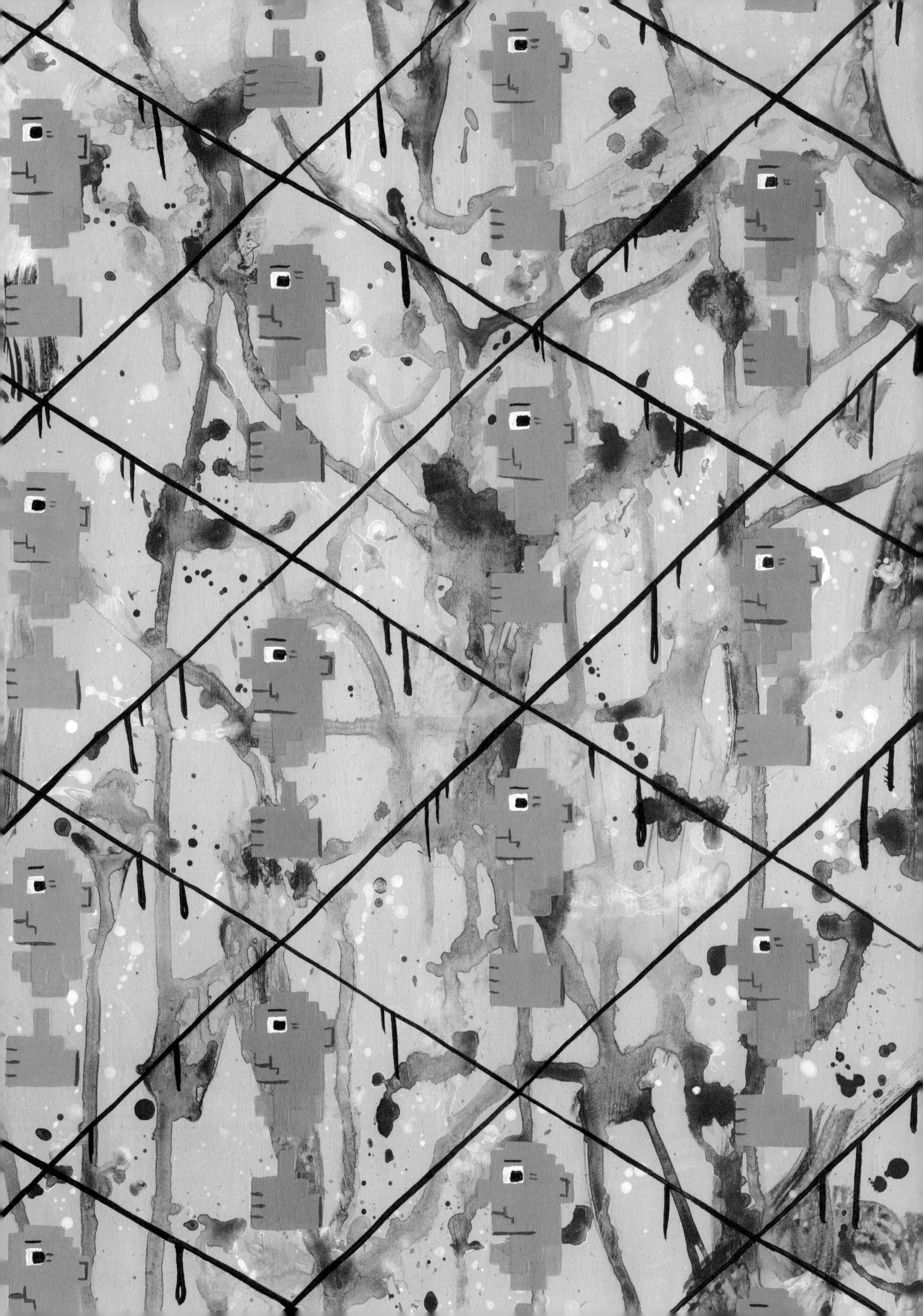

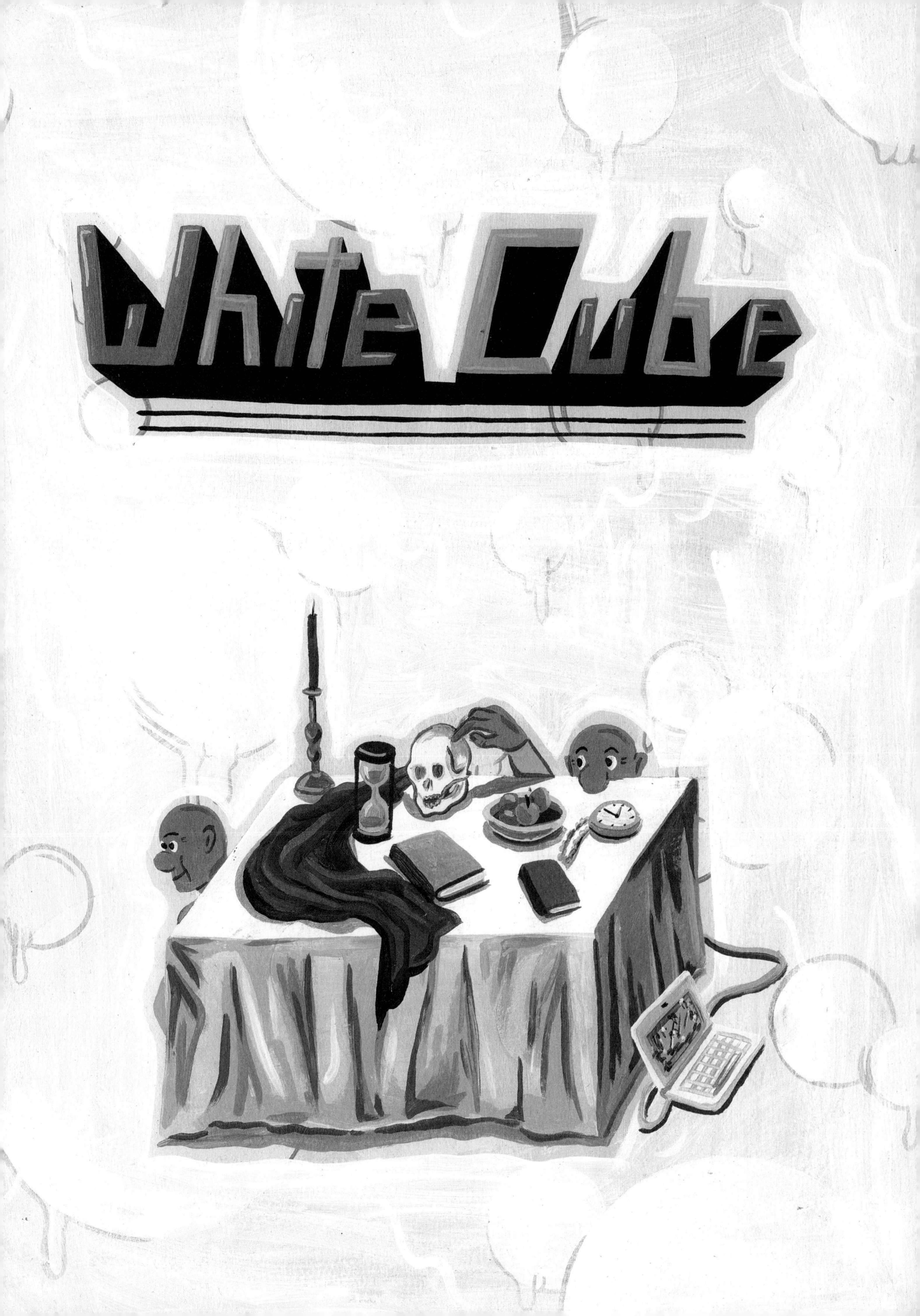
White Cube

FOR HANNELORE VAN DIJCH & BRECHT EVENS

WWW.DRAWNANDQUARTERLY.COM

FIRST HARDCOVER EDITION: FEBRUARY 2014
ISBN 978-1-77046-139-0
PRINTED IN CHINA
10 9 8 7 6 5 4 3 2 1

LIBRARY AND ARCHIVES CANADA CATALOGUING IN PUBLICATION:
VANDENBROUCHE, BRECHT, AUTHOR, ARTIST
     WHITE CUBE / BRECHT VANDENBROUCHE
ISBN 978-1-77046-139-0 (BOUND)
1.GRAPHIC NOVELS 1.TITLE
PN6790.B43V335 2014   741.5'9493   C2013-902775-0

PUBLISHED IN THE USA BY DRAWN & QUARTERLY, A CLIENT PUBLISHER OF
FARRAR, STRAUS AND GIROUX. 18 WEST 18TH STREET, NEW YORK, NY 10011.
ORDERS: 888.330.8477.

PUBLISHED IN CANADA BY DRAWN & QUARTERLY, A CLIENT PUBLISHER OF
RAINCOAST BOOKS. 2240 VIKING WAY, RICHMOND, BC V6V 1N2.
ORDERS: 800.663.5714.

PUBLISHED IN THE UNITED KINGDOM BY DRAWN & QUARTERLY, A CLIENT PUBLISHER OF
PUBLISHERS GROUP UK. 63-66 HATTON GARDEN, LONDON, EC1N8LE.
ORDERS: INFO@PGUK.CO.UK.

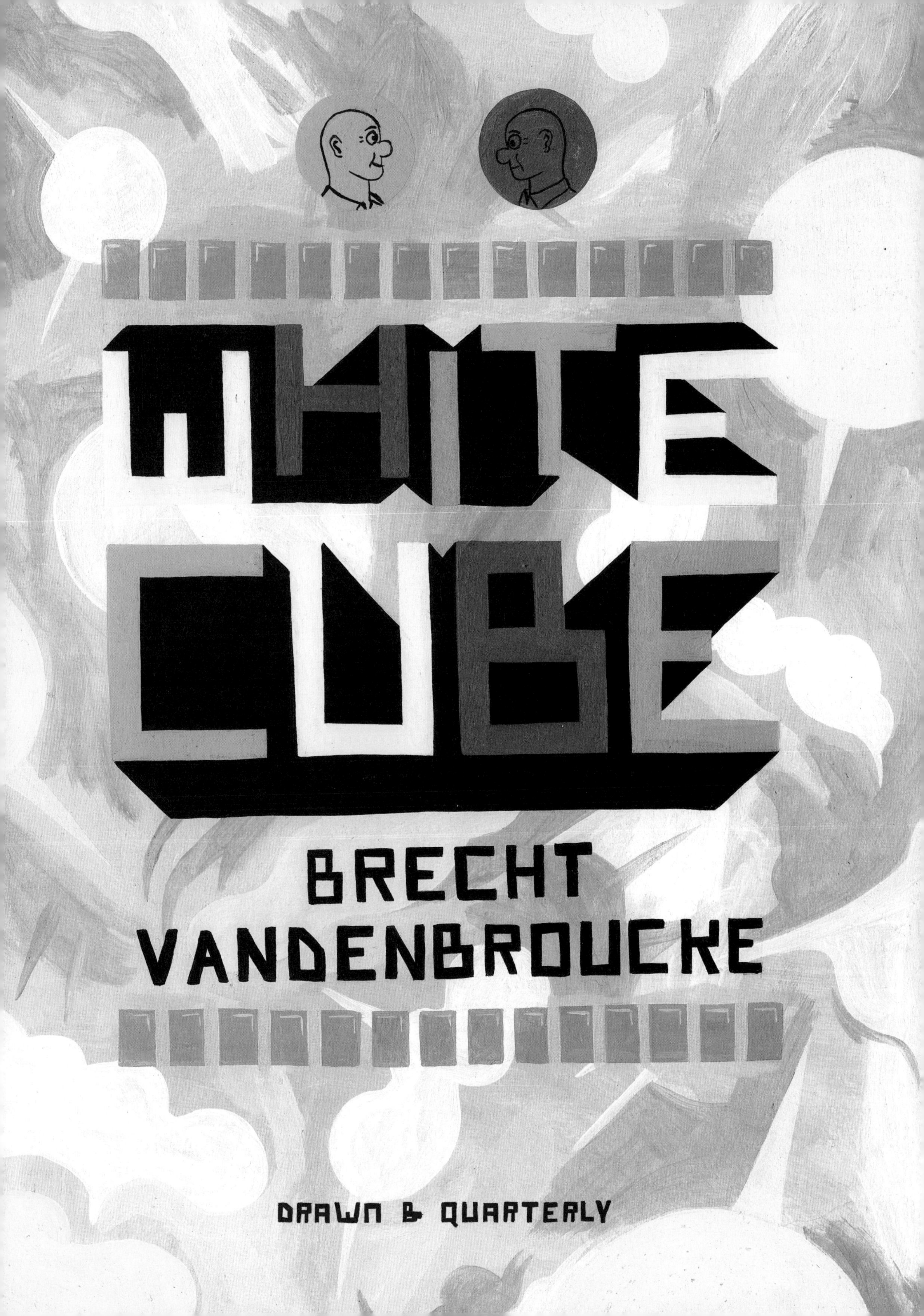
WHITE CUBE
BRECHT VANDENBROUCKE
DRAWN & QUARTERLY

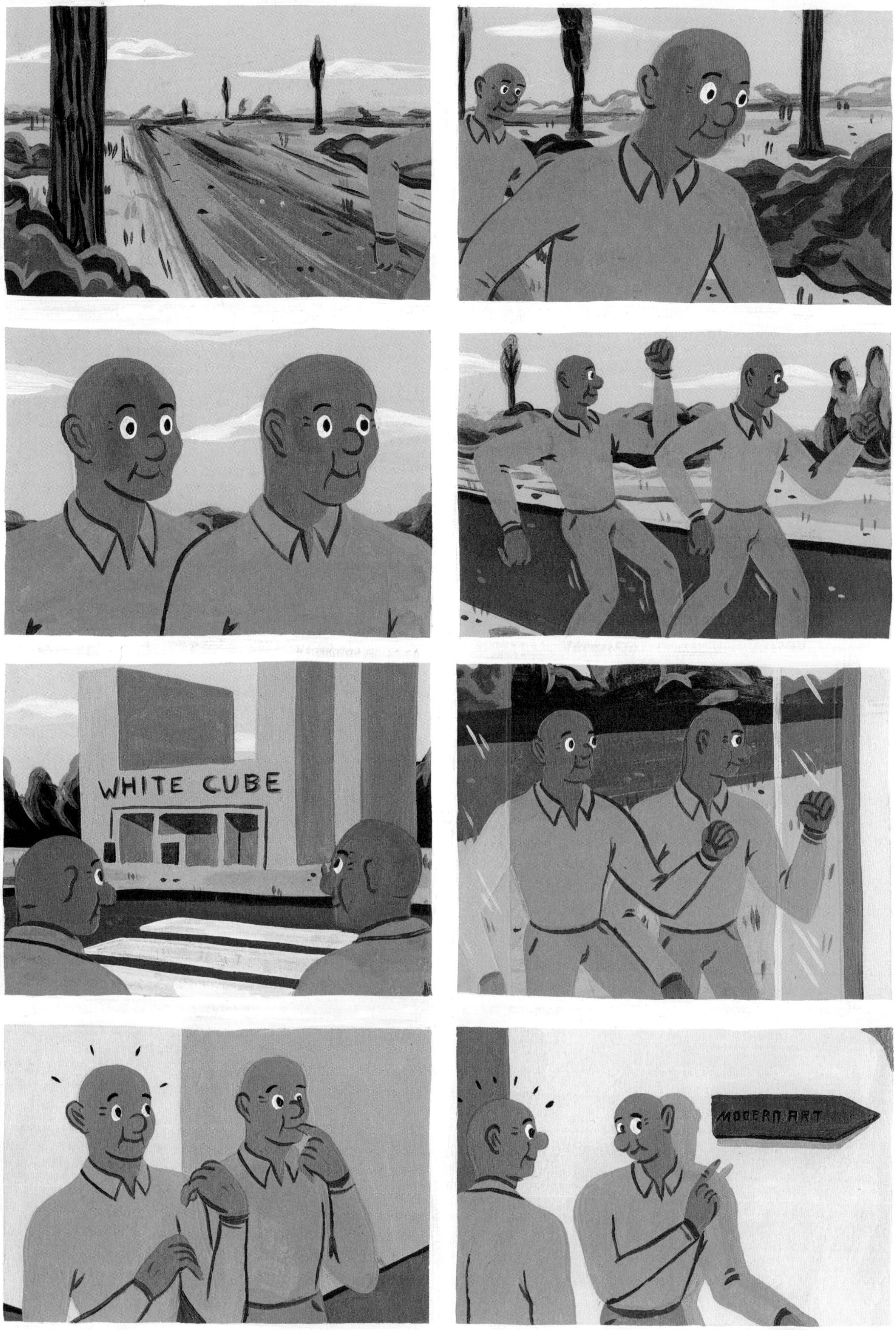
WHITE CUBE
MODERN ART

MODERN ART
MODERN ART
MODERN ART
MODERN ART
MODERN ART
MODERN ART
MODERN ART
MODERN ART

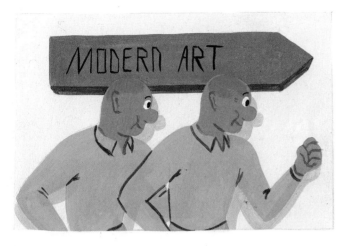

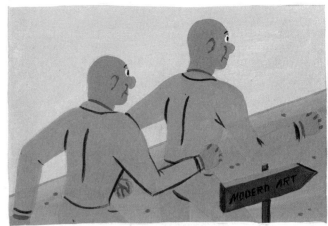

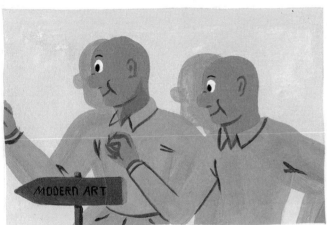

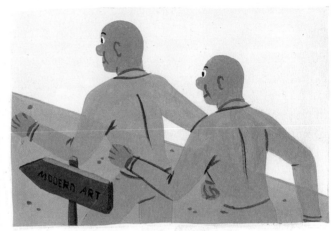

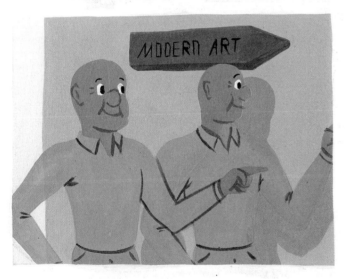

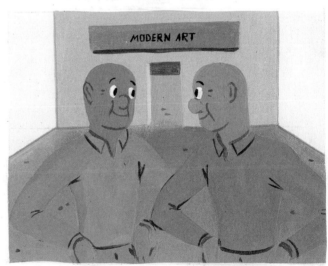

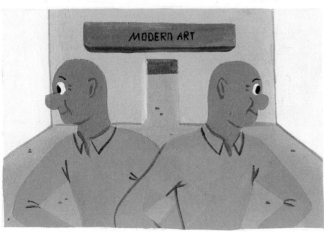

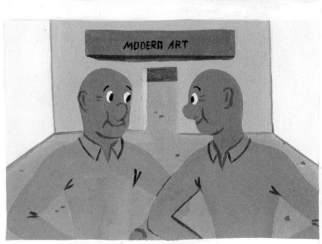

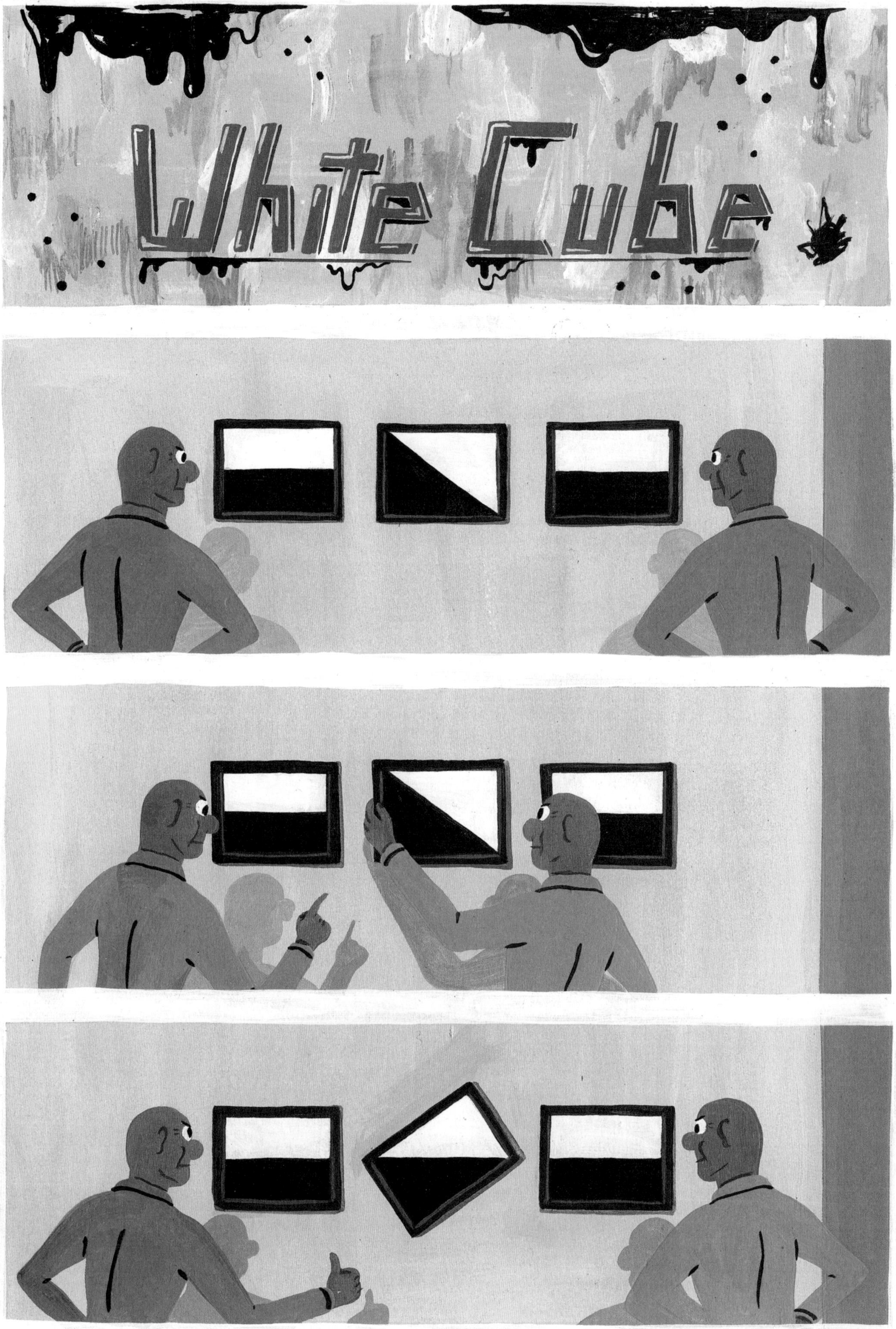
White Cube

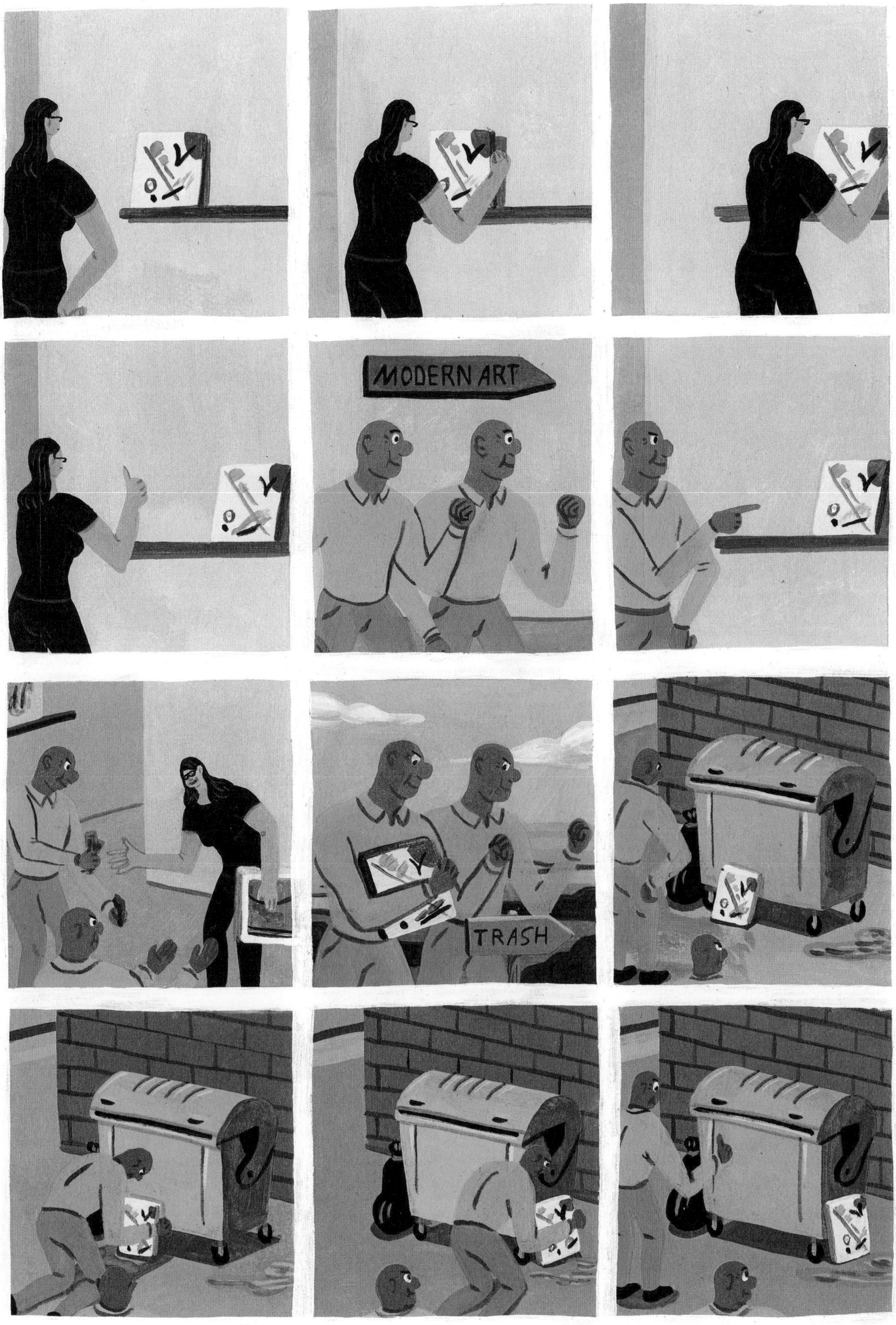
MODERN ART
TRASH

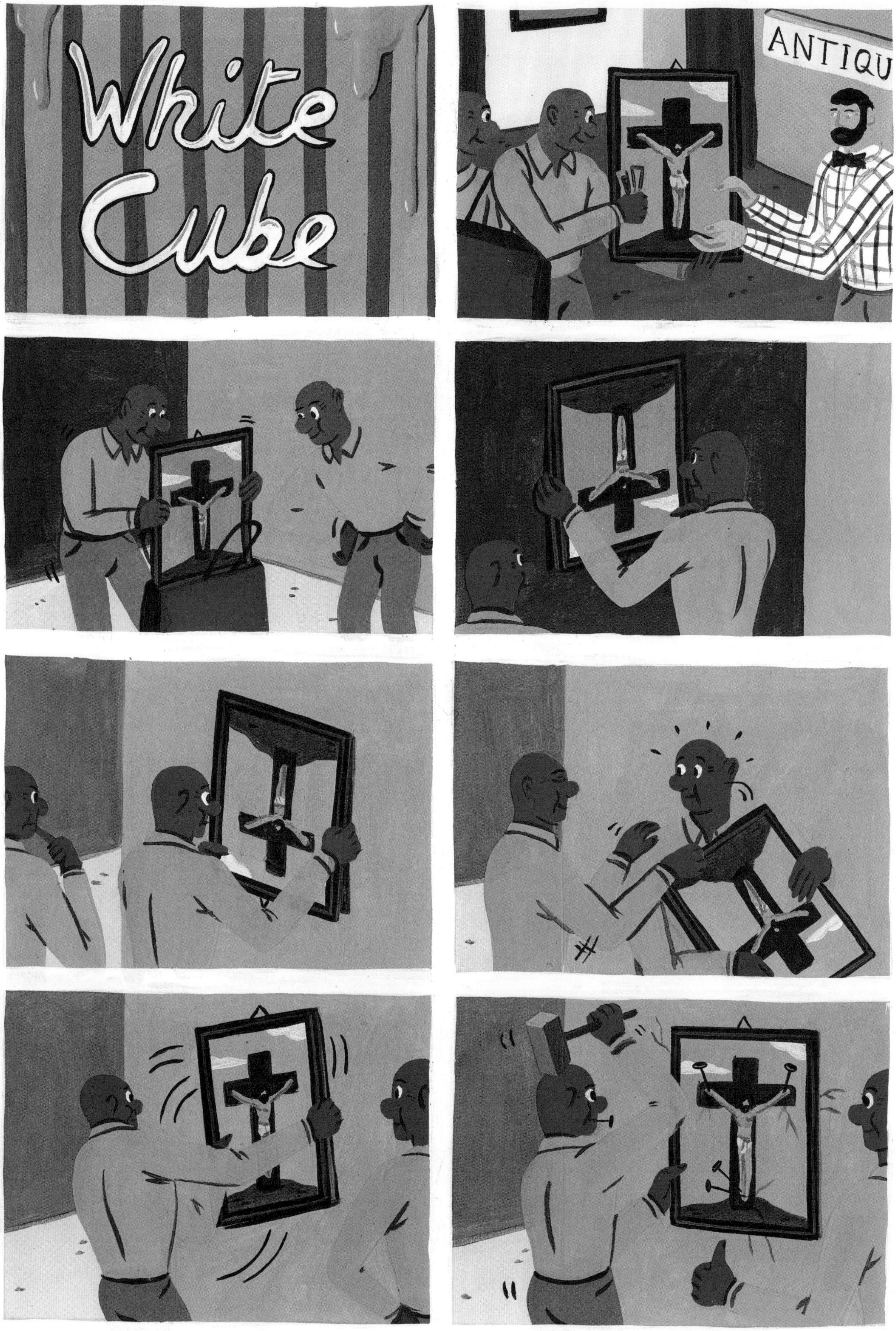
White Cube
ANTIQU

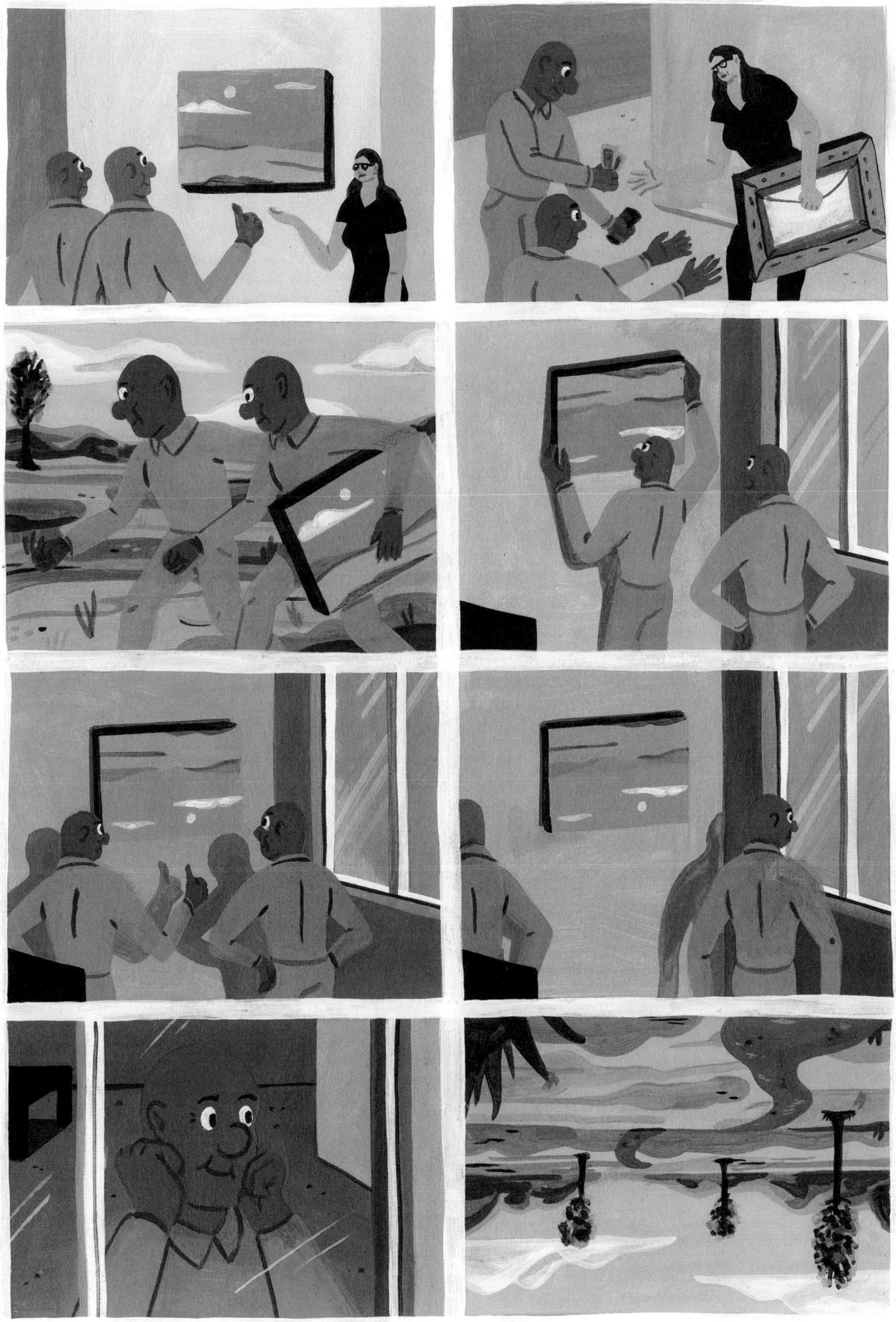

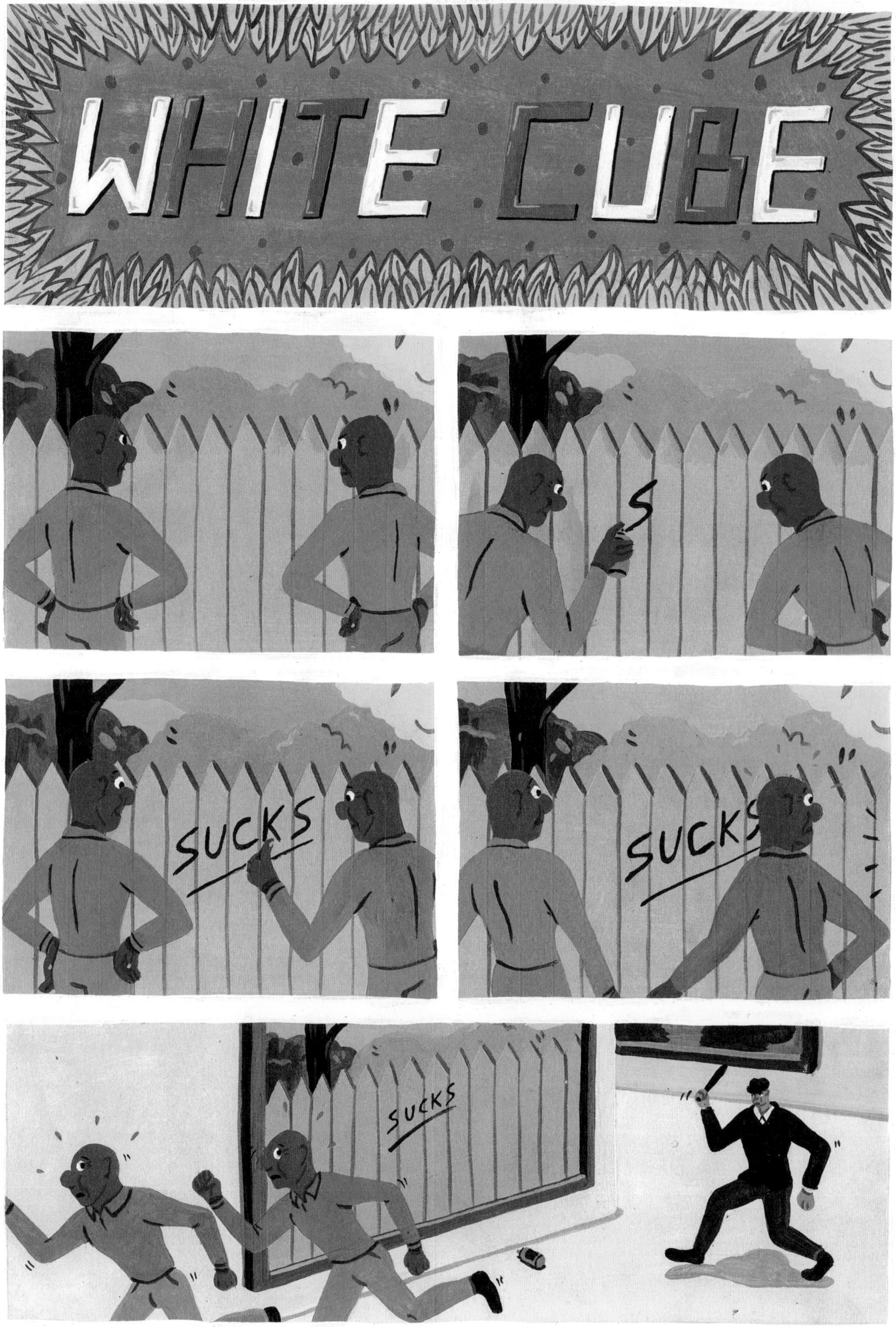
WHITE CUBE
S
SUCKS
SUCKS
SUCKS

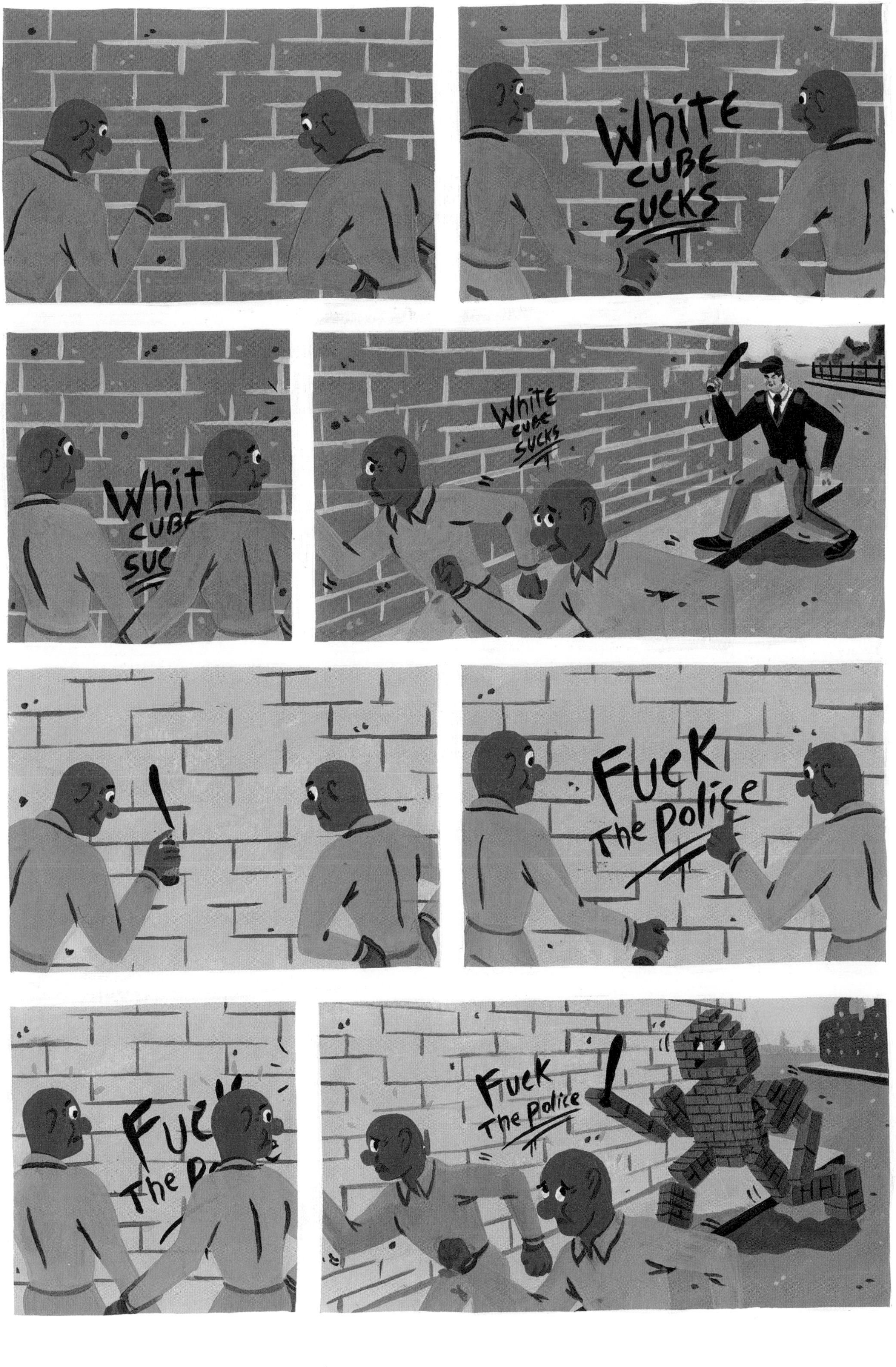
White CUBE SUCKS
White CUBE SUCKS
Fuck The police
Fuck The police

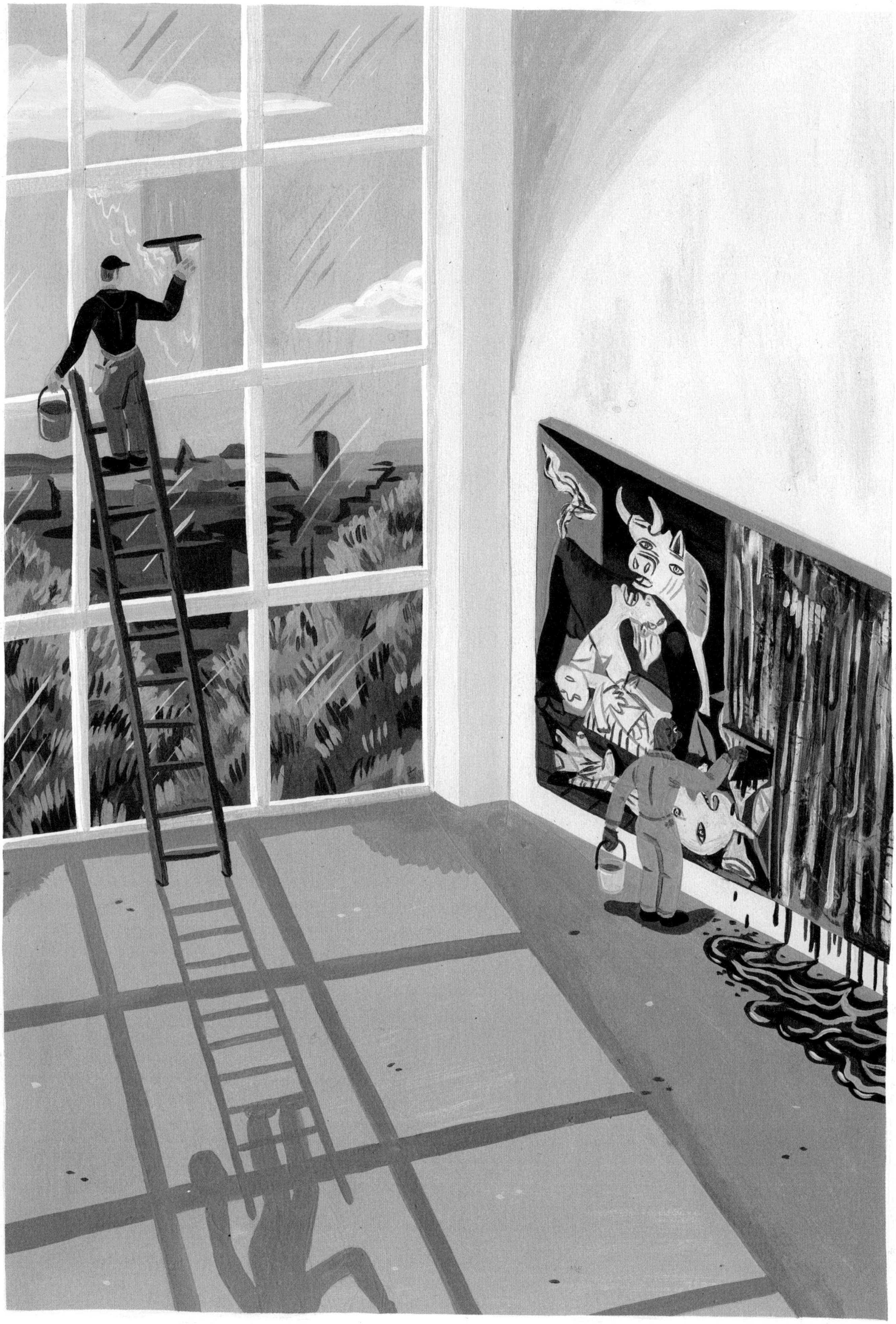

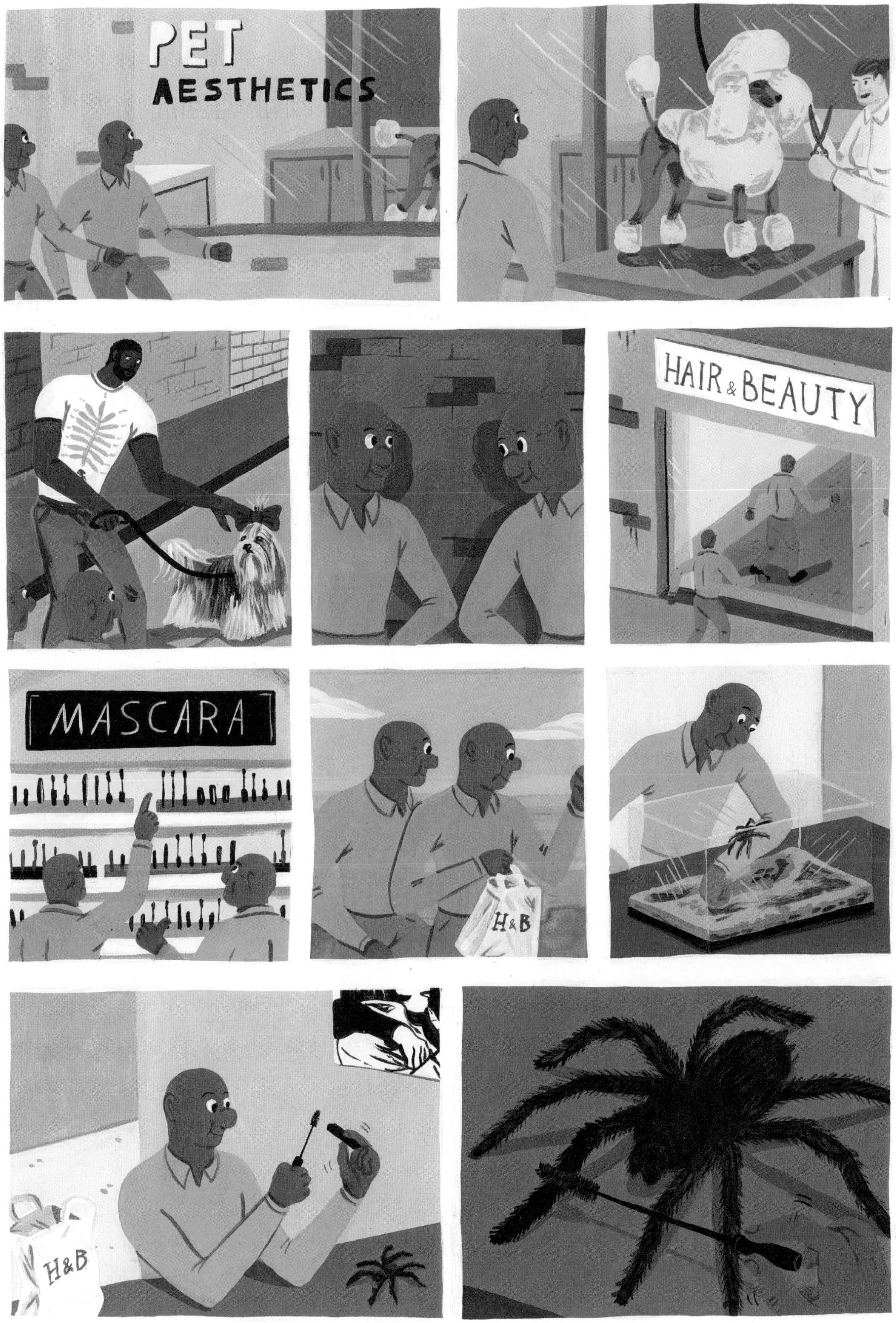
PET
AESTHETICS
HAIR & BEAUTY
MASCARA
H&B
H&B
H&B

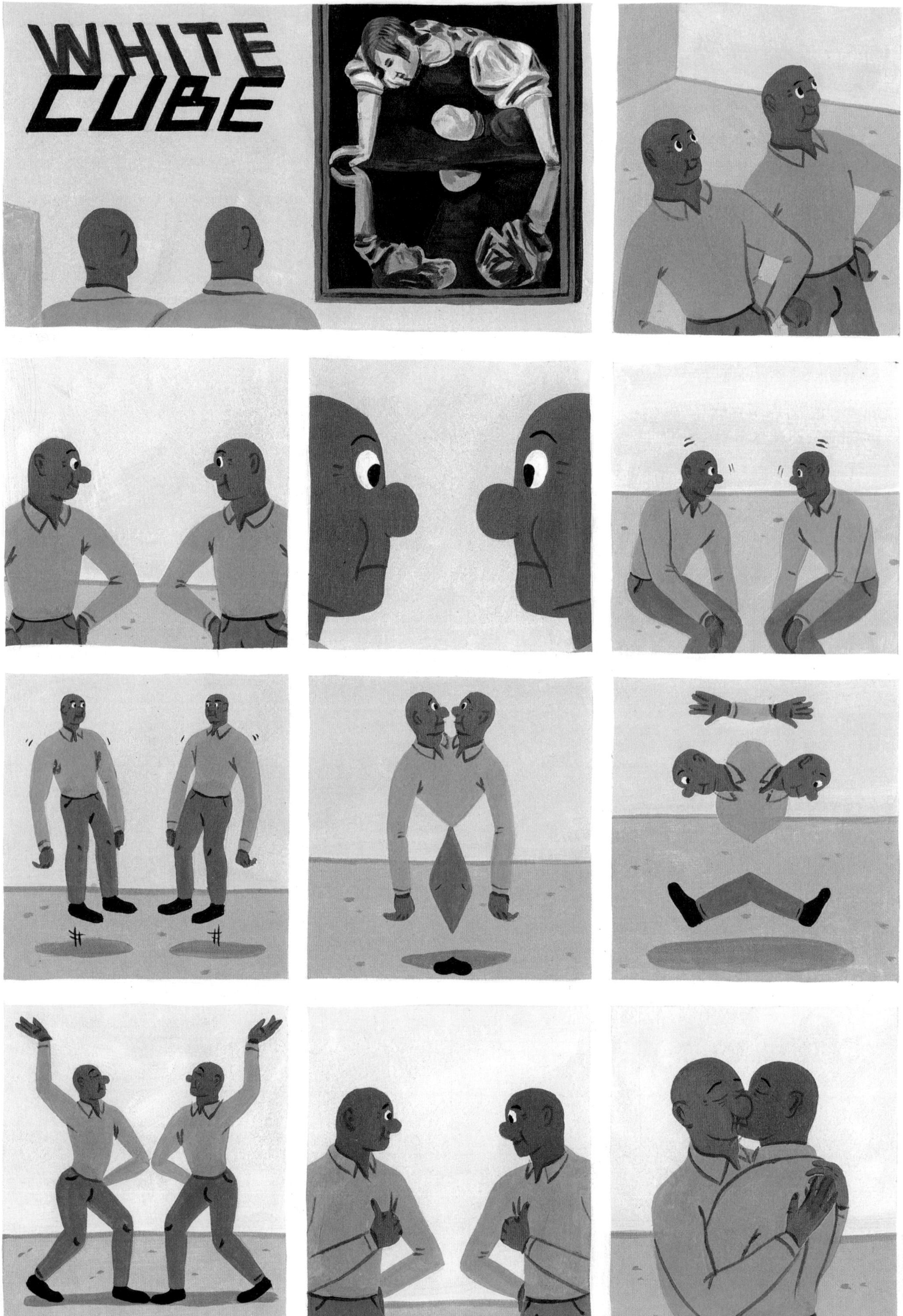
WHITE CUBE

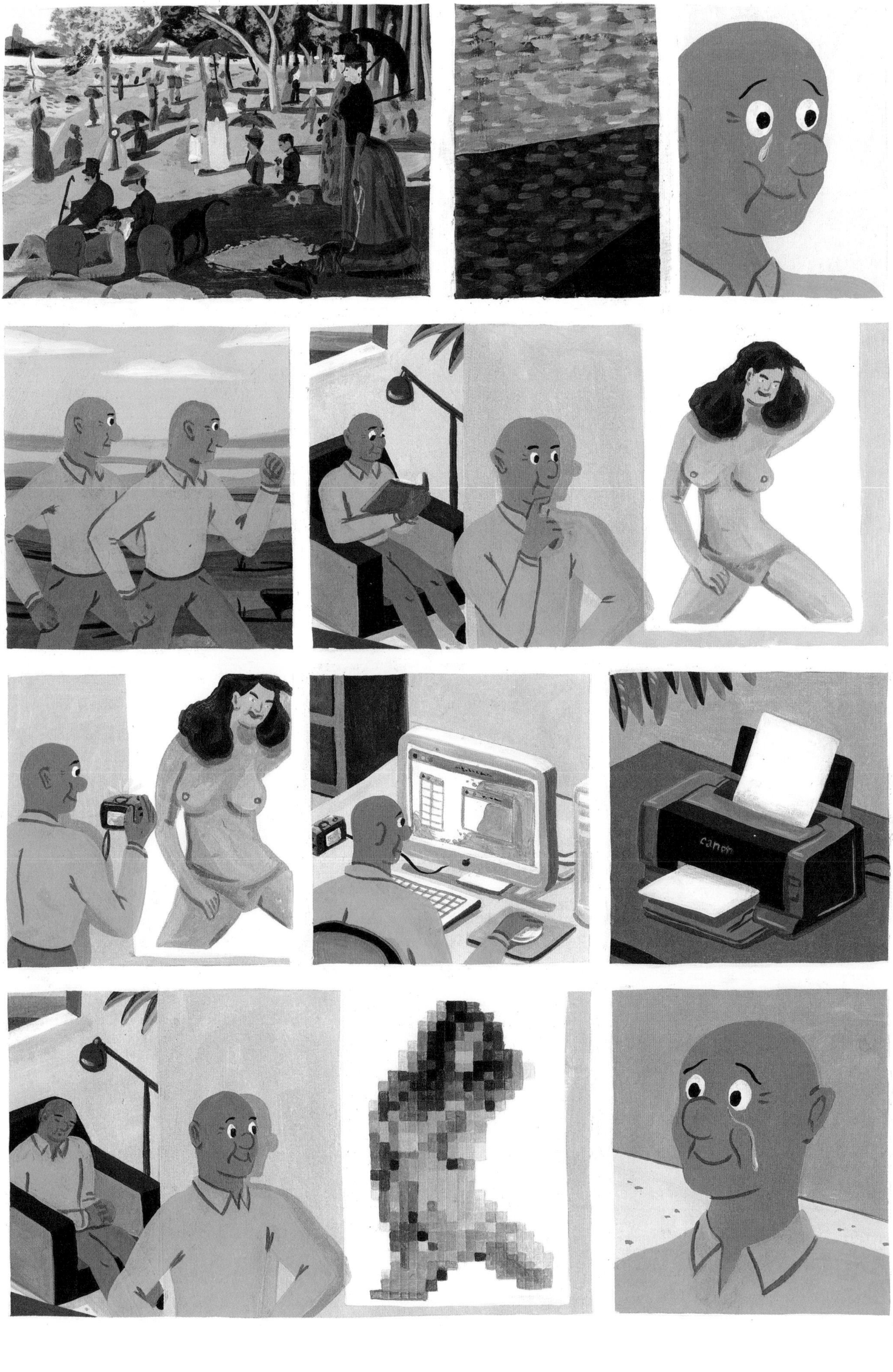
canon

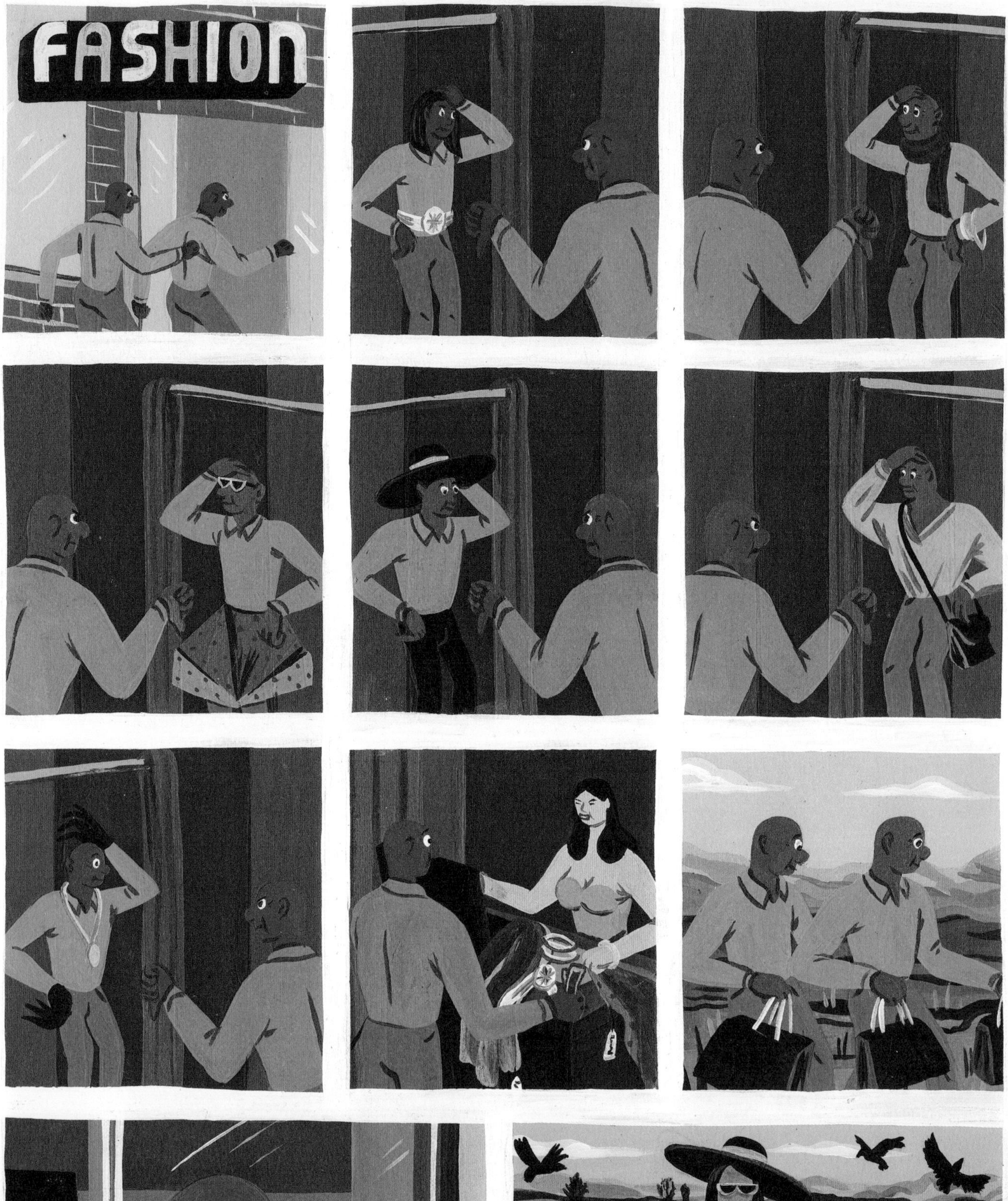
FASHION

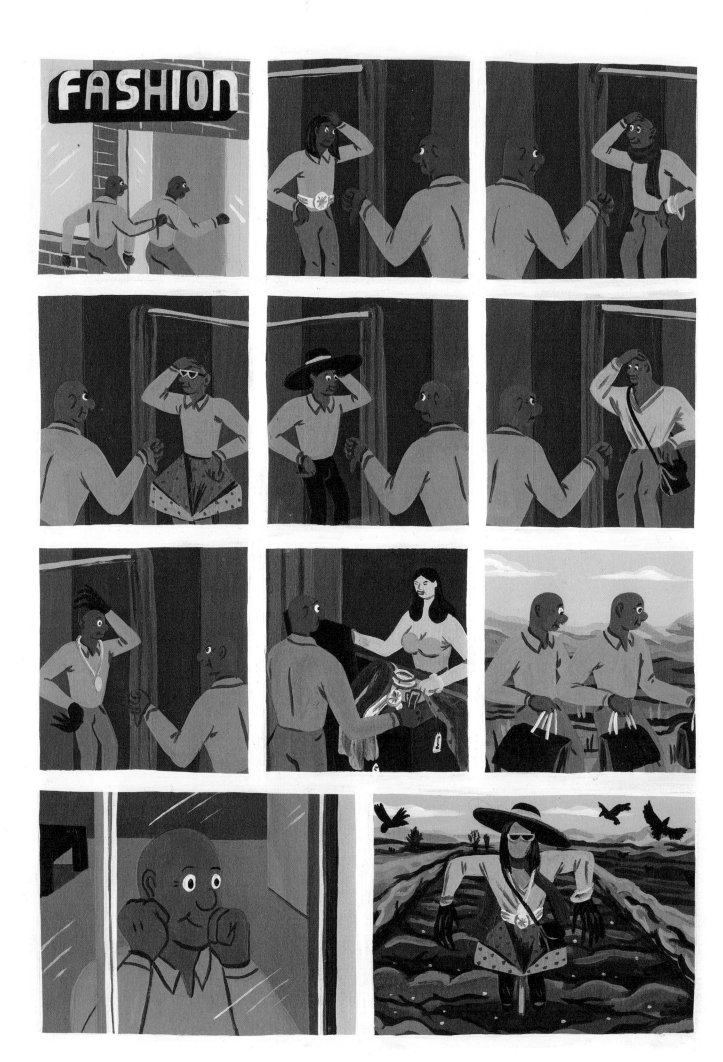

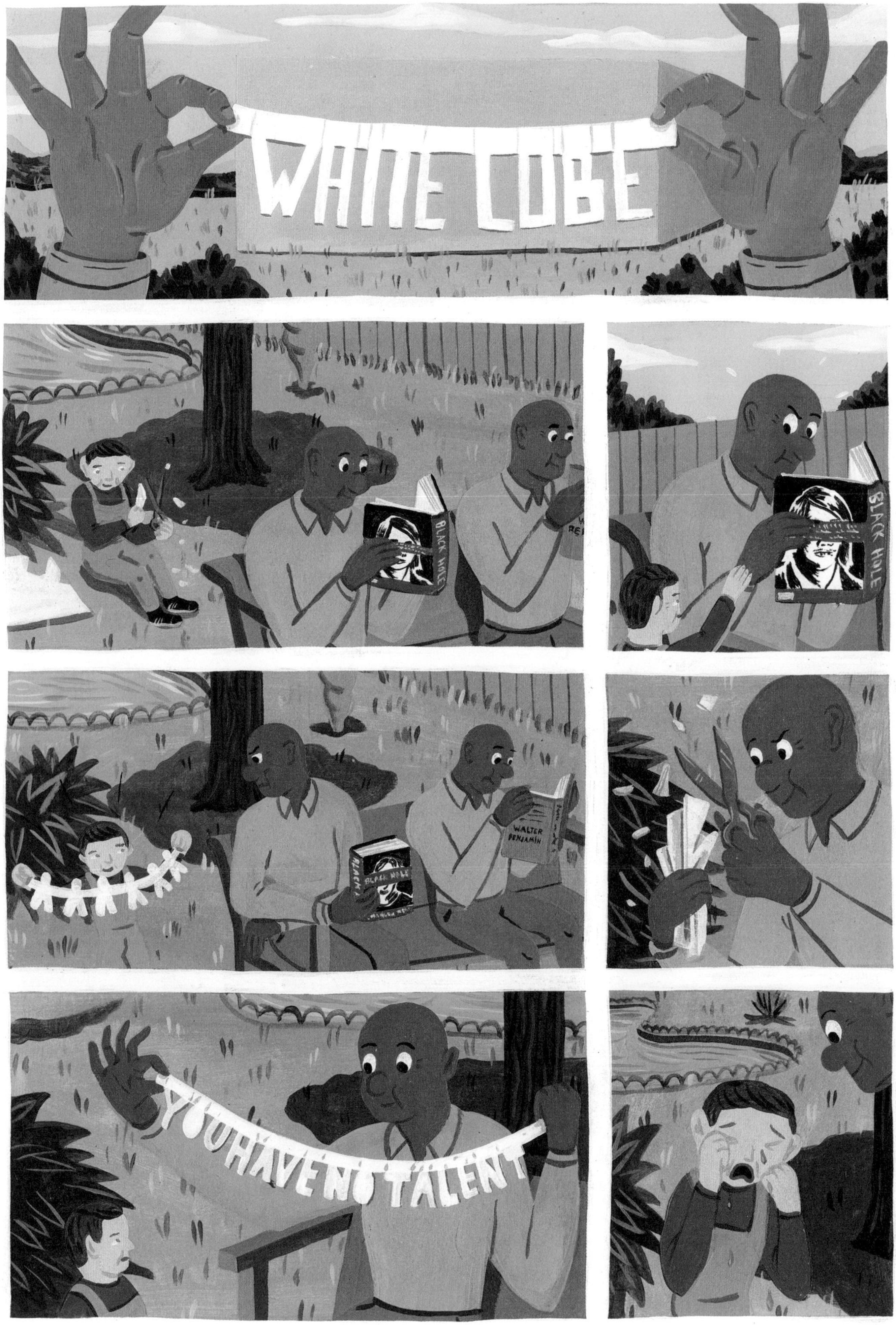
WHITE CUBE
BLACK HOLE
BLACK HOLE
BLACK HOLE
WALTER BENJAMIN
YOU HAVE NO TALENT

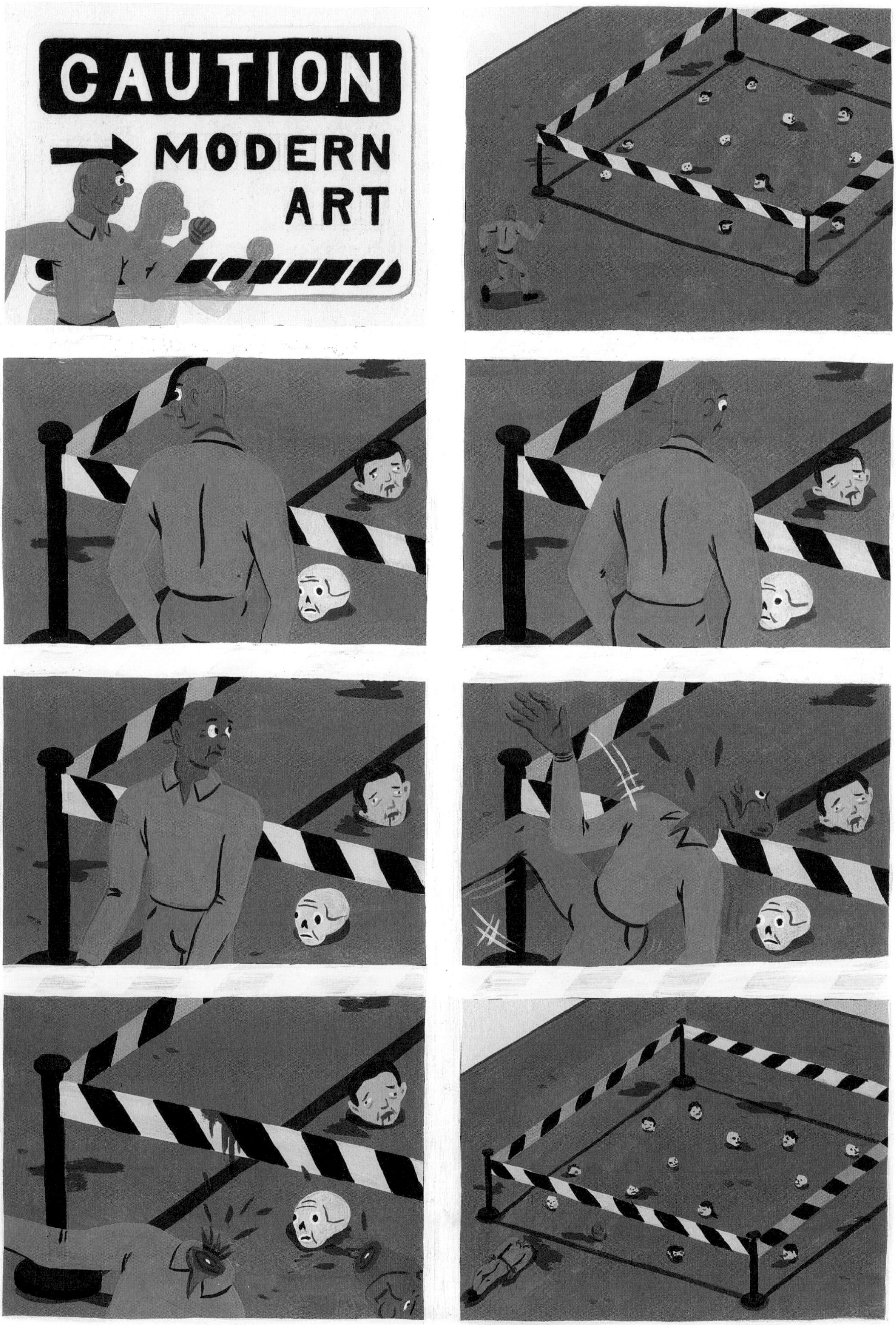
CAUTION
MODERN
ART

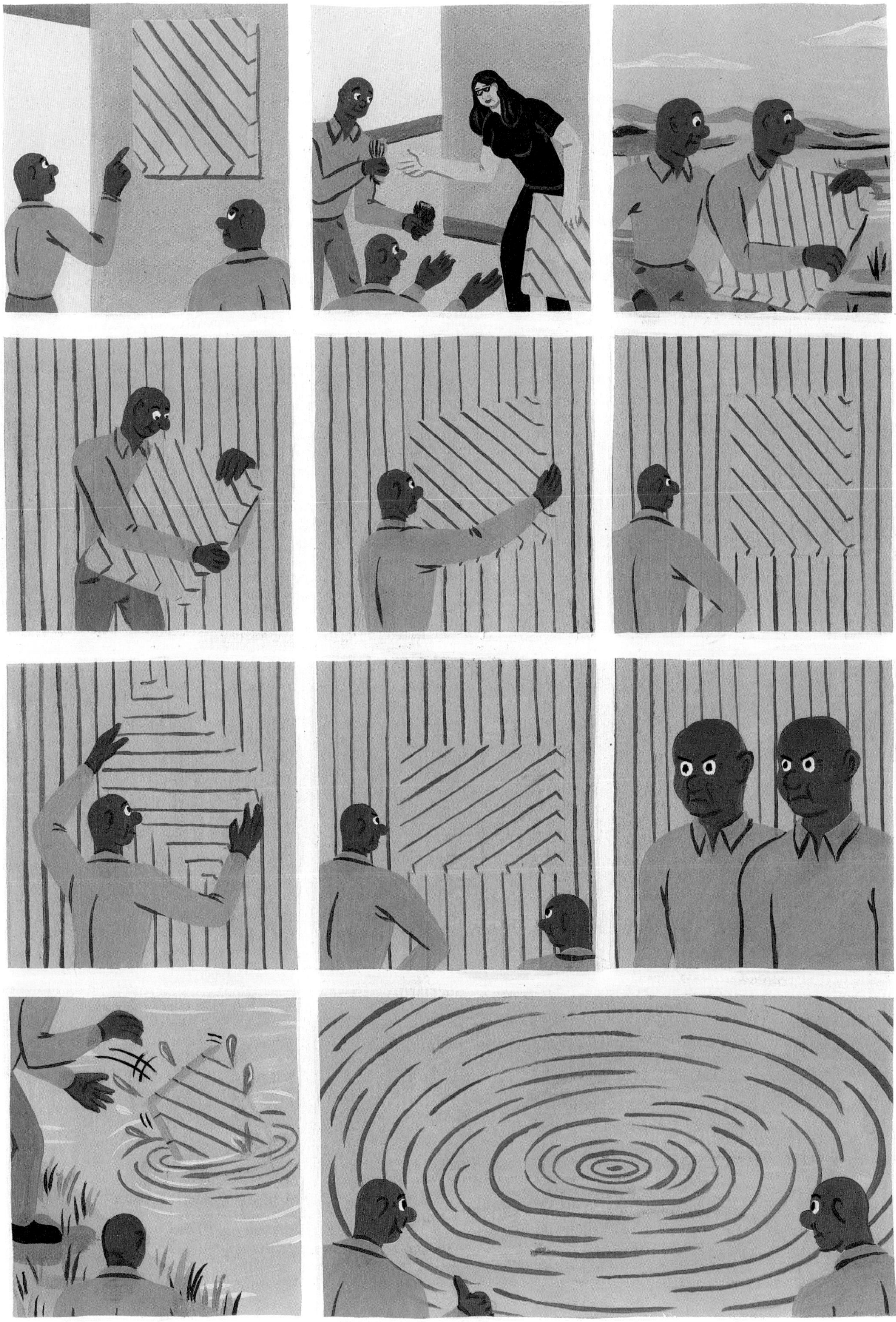

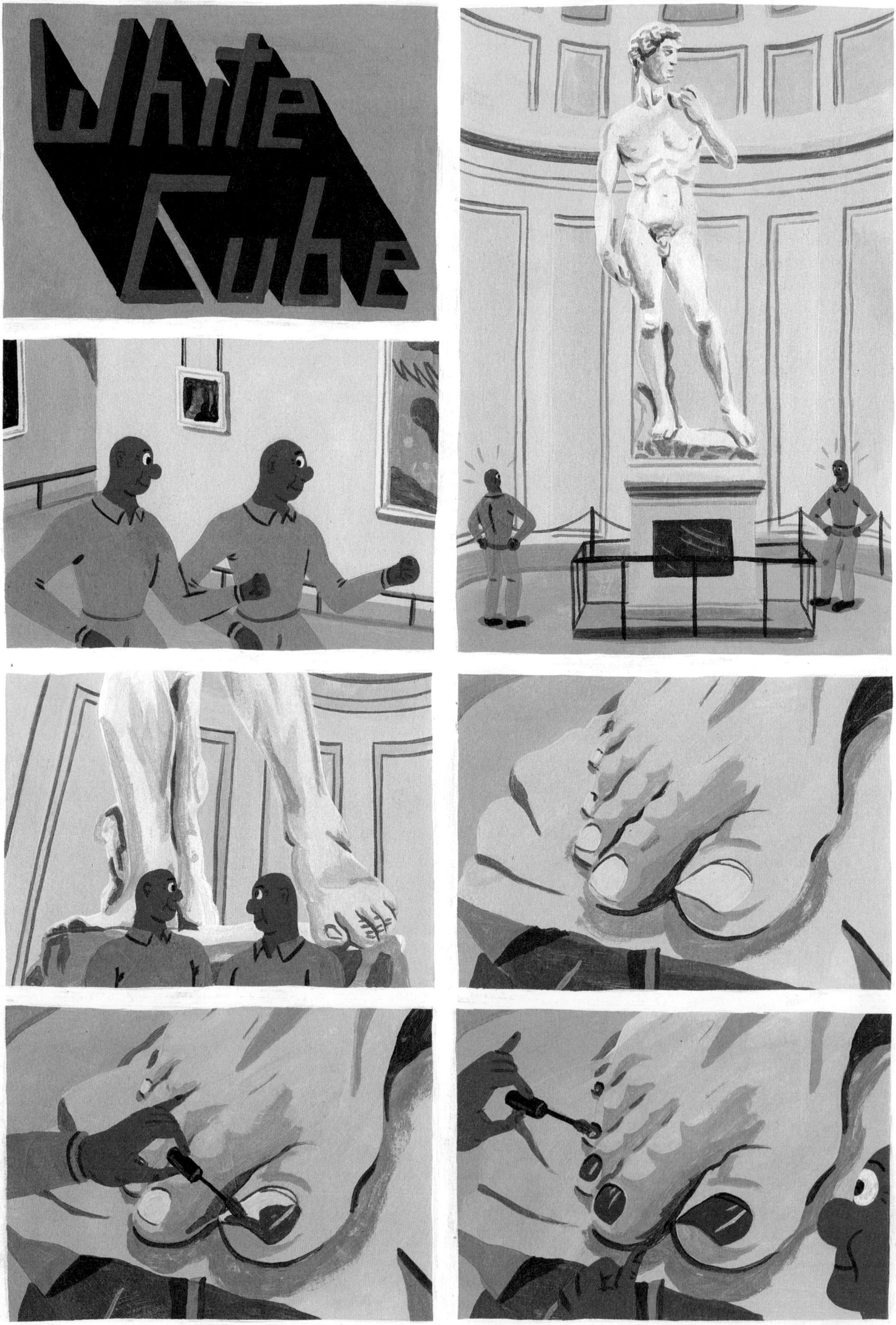
White Cube

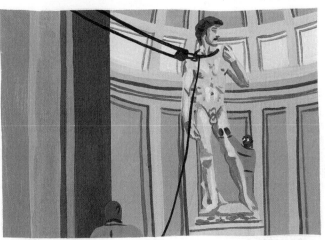

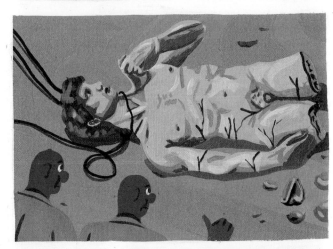

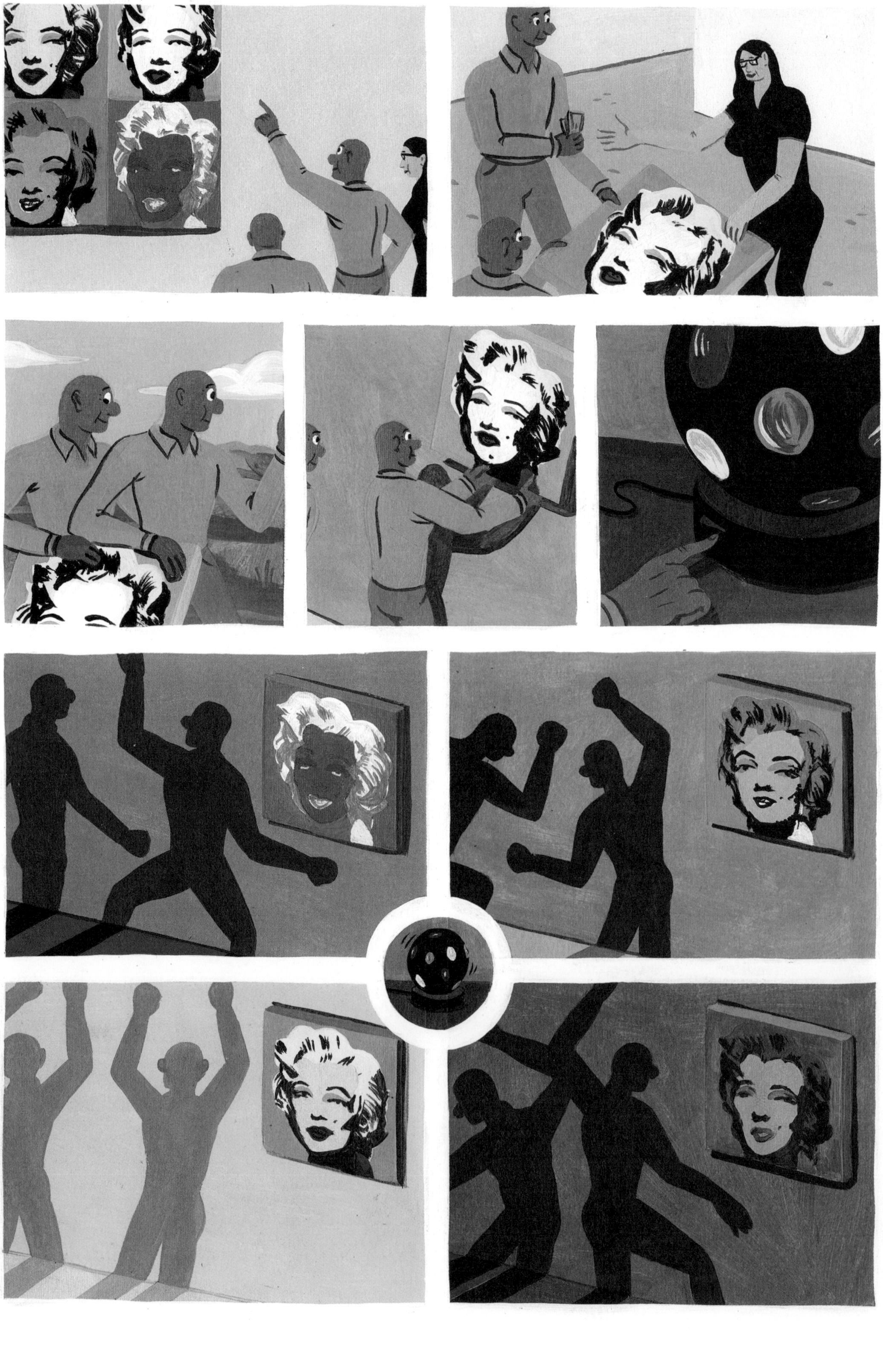

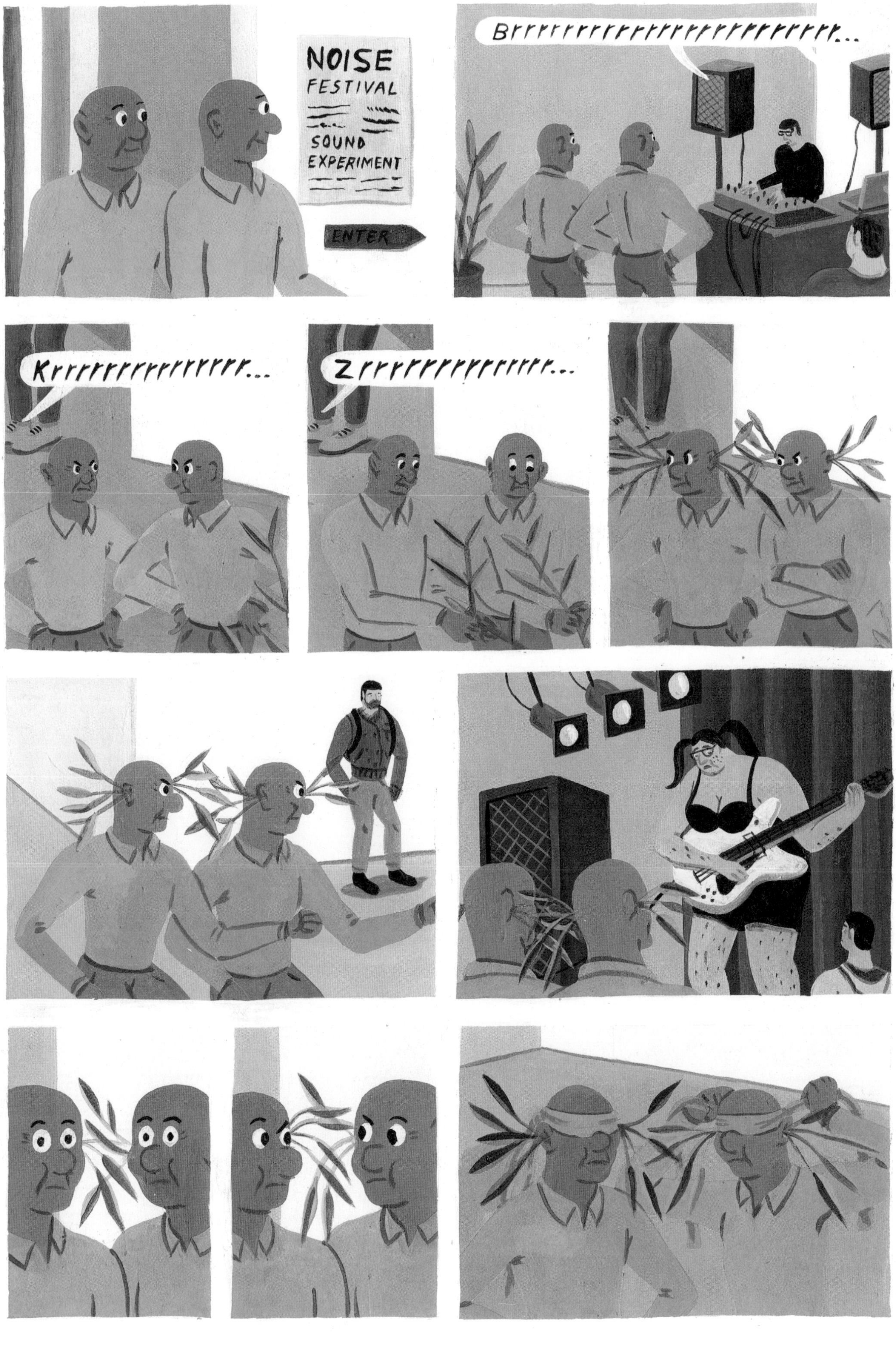
NOISE
FESTIVAL
SOUND
EXPERIMENT
ENTER
Brrrrrrrrrrrrrrrrrrrrrrrrrr...
Krrrrrrrrrrrrrrr...
Zrrrrrrrrrrrrrrr...

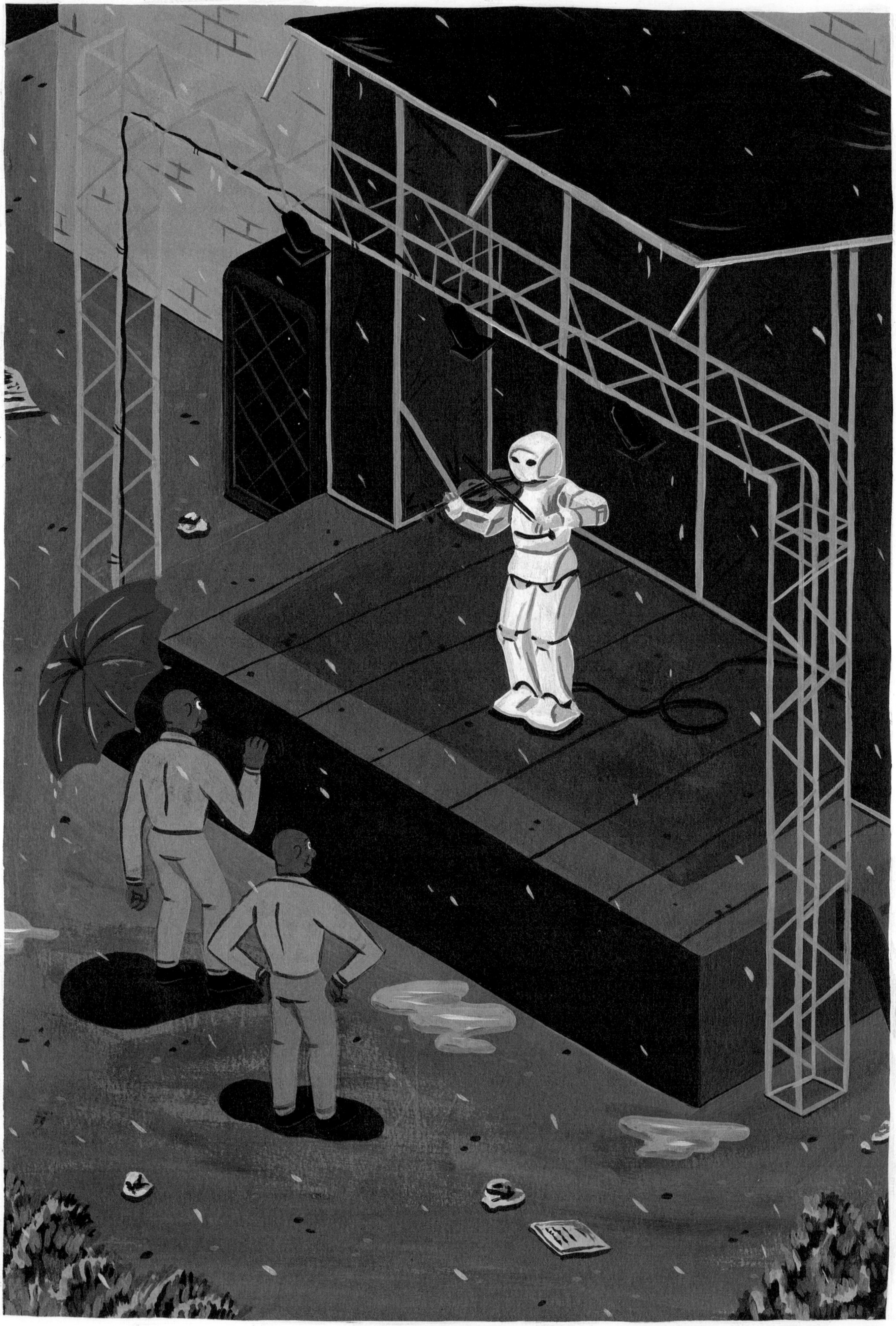

WHITE CUBE

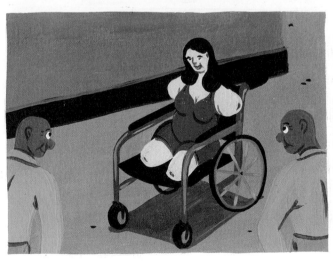

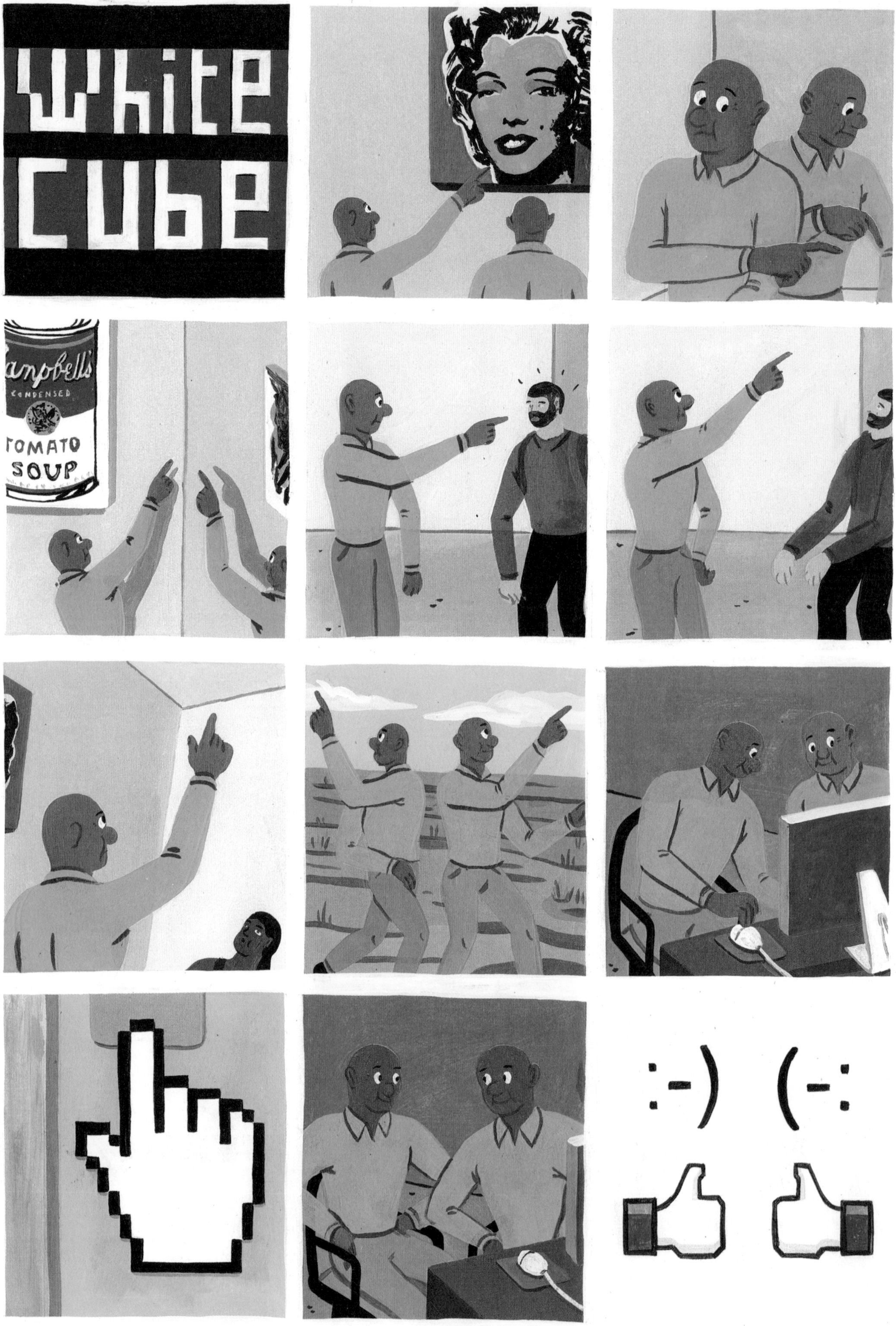
White Cube
Campbell's
CONDENSED
TOMATO SOUP
:-) (-:

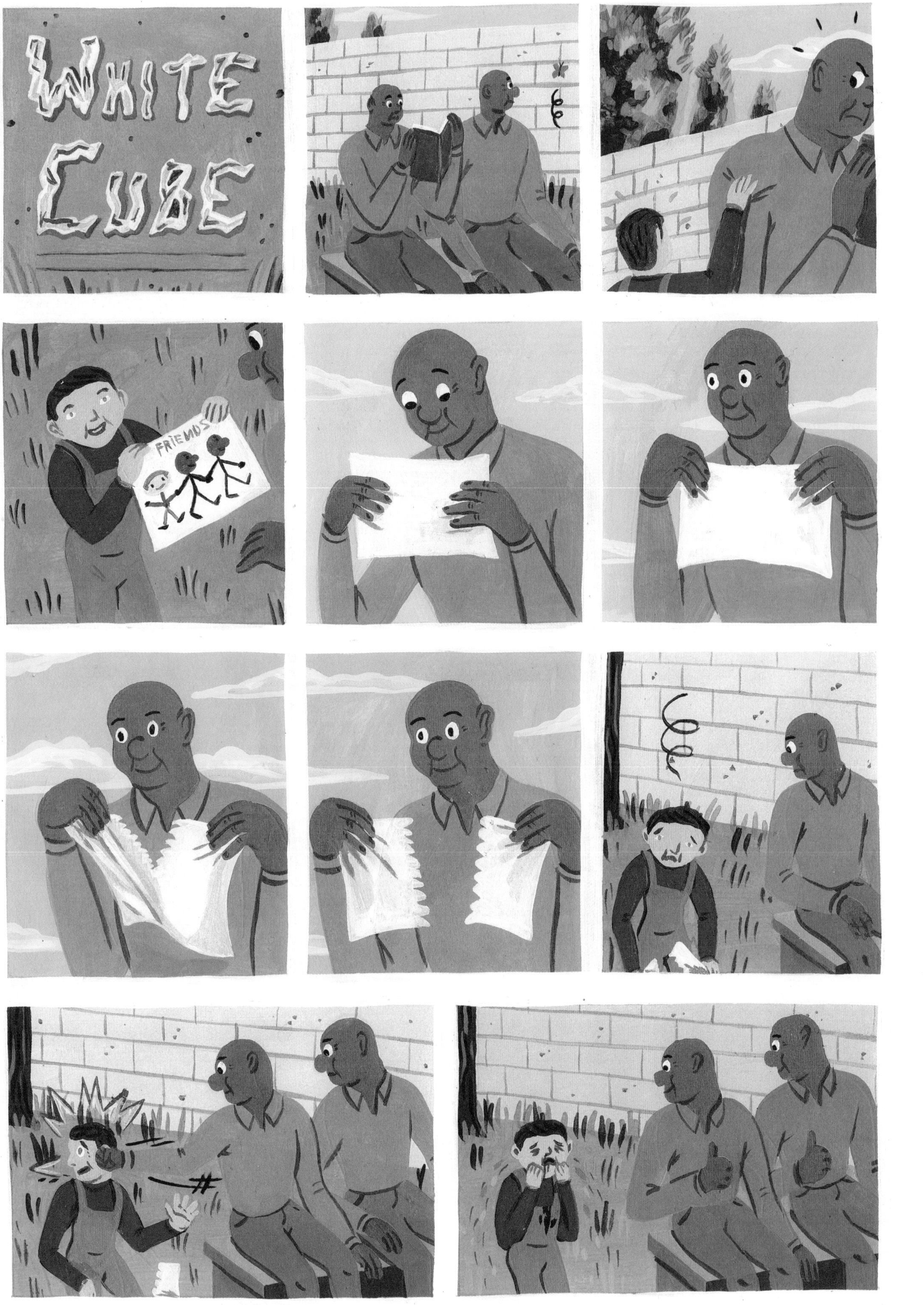
WHITE CUBE
FRIENDS

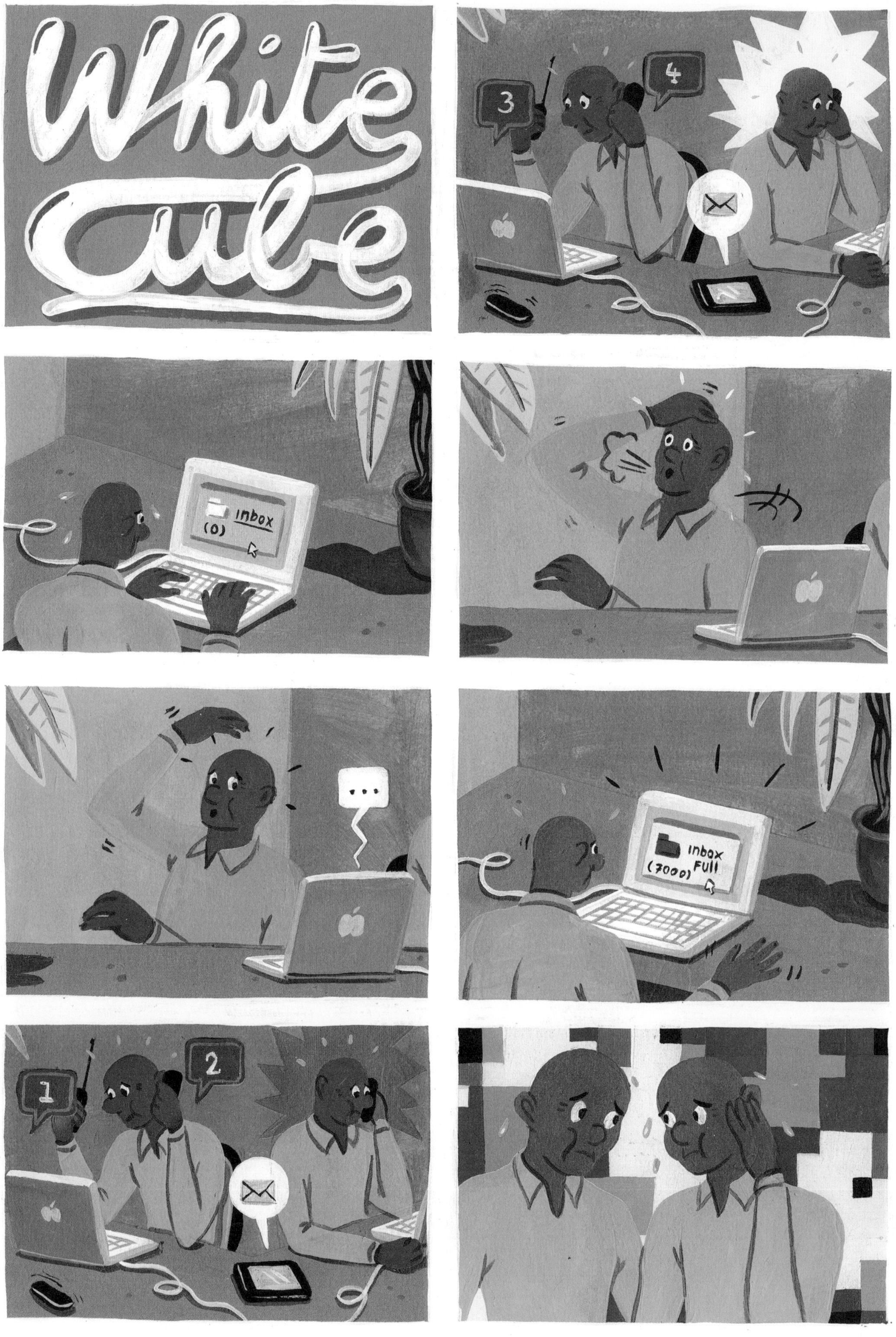
White
Cube
3
4
inbox
(0)
inbox
Full
(7000)
1
2

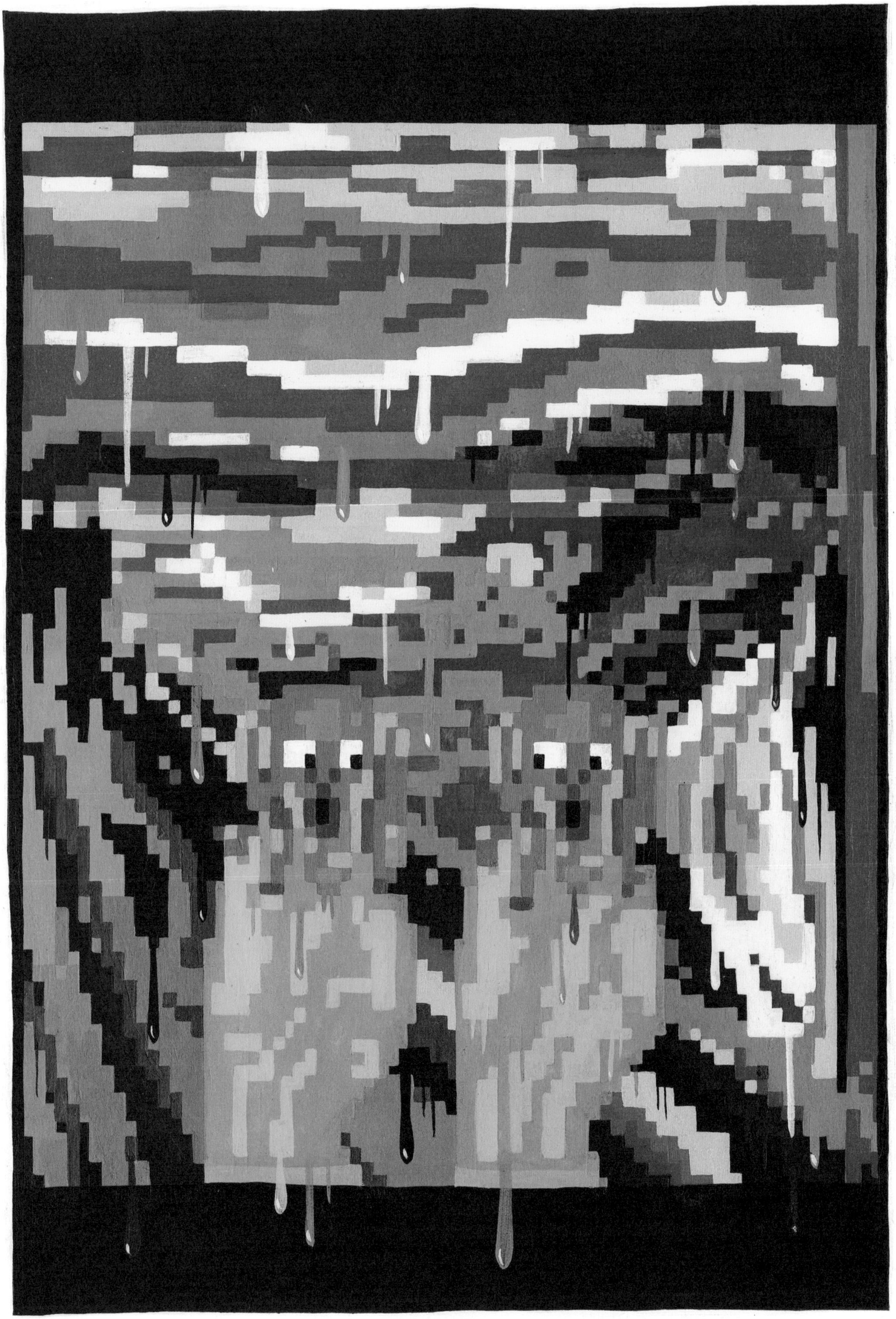

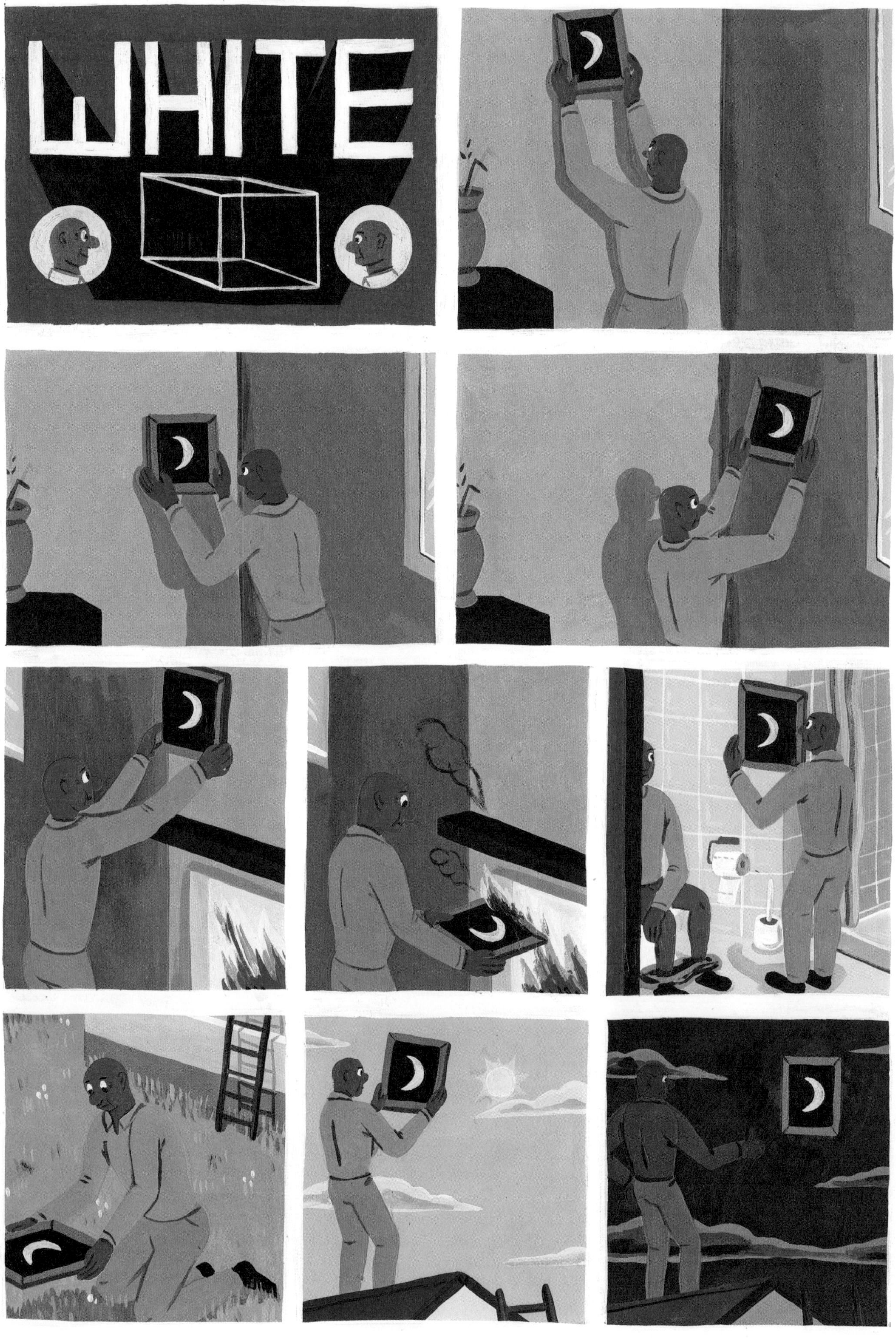
WHITE

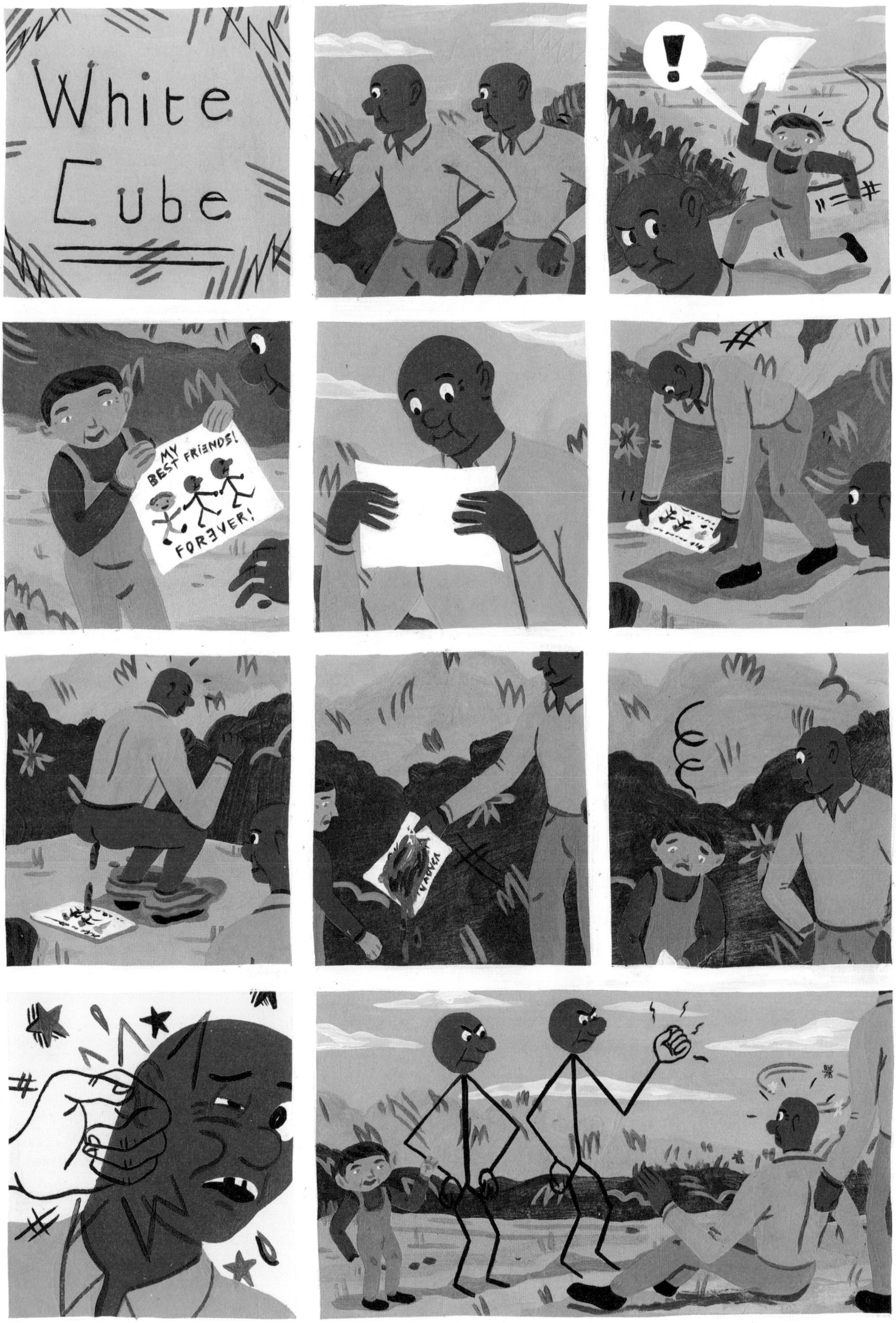
White Cube
!
MY BEST FRIENDS!
FOREVER!

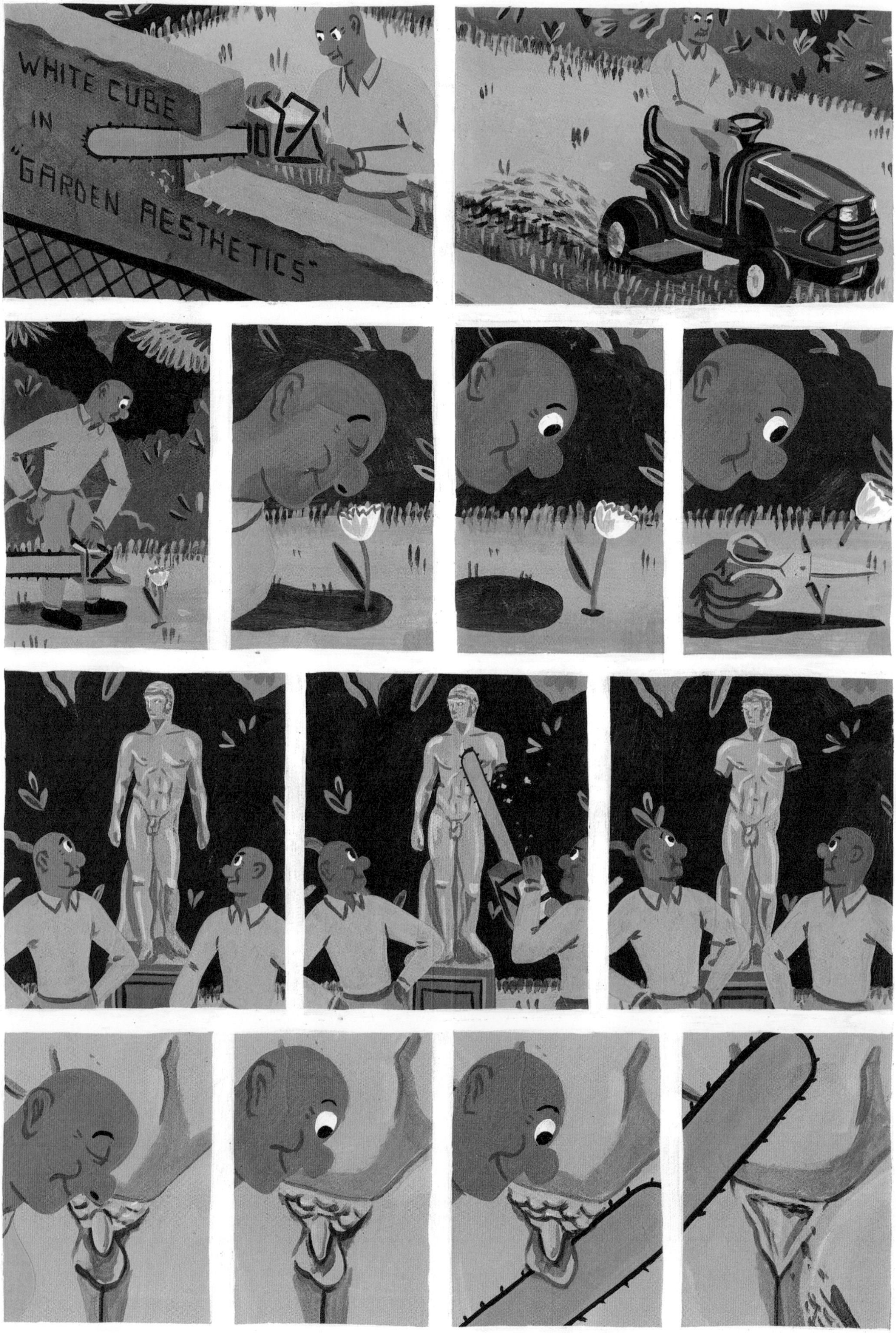
WHITE CUBE
IN
"GARDEN AESTHETICS"

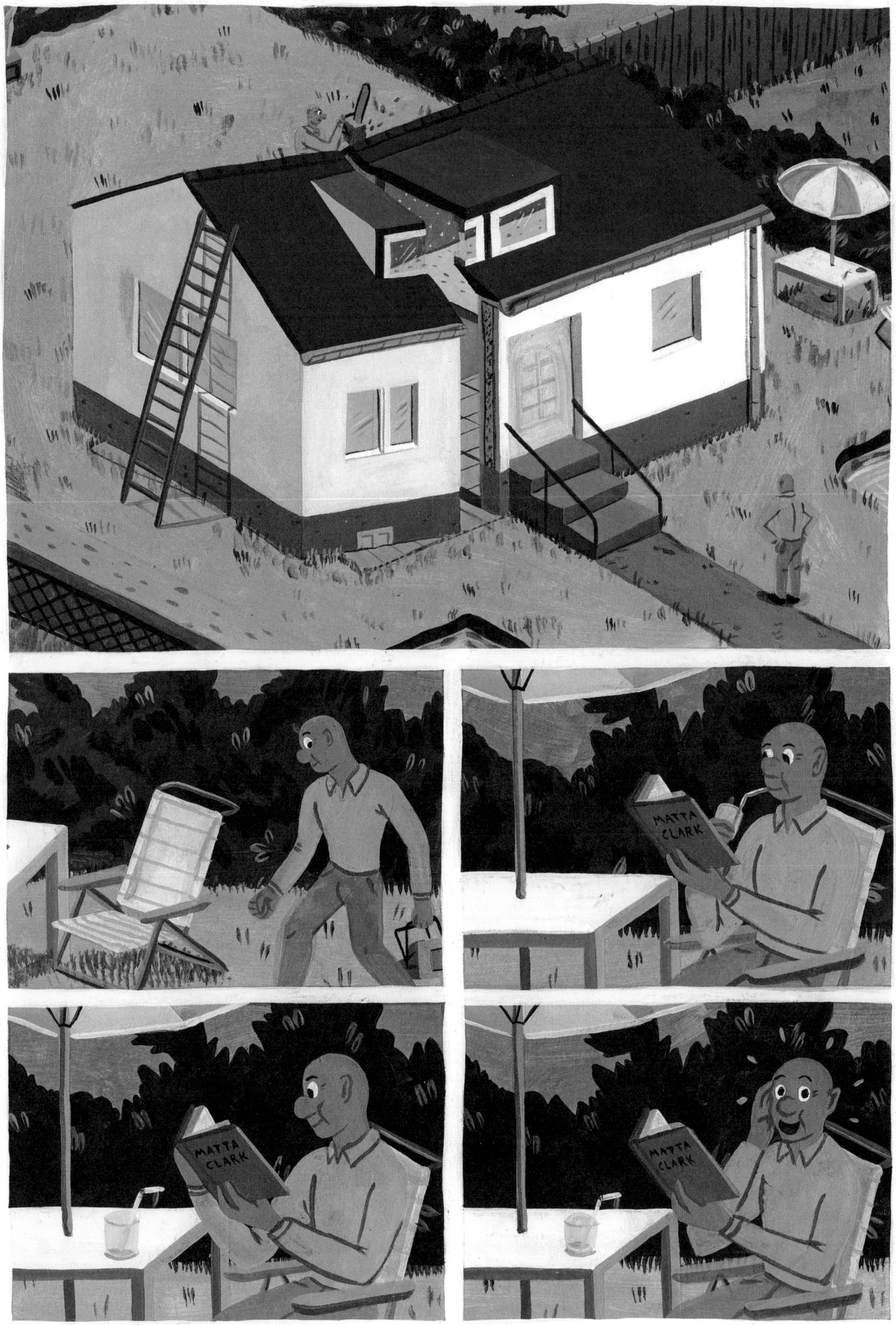
MATTA CLARK
MATTA CLARK
MATTA CLARK

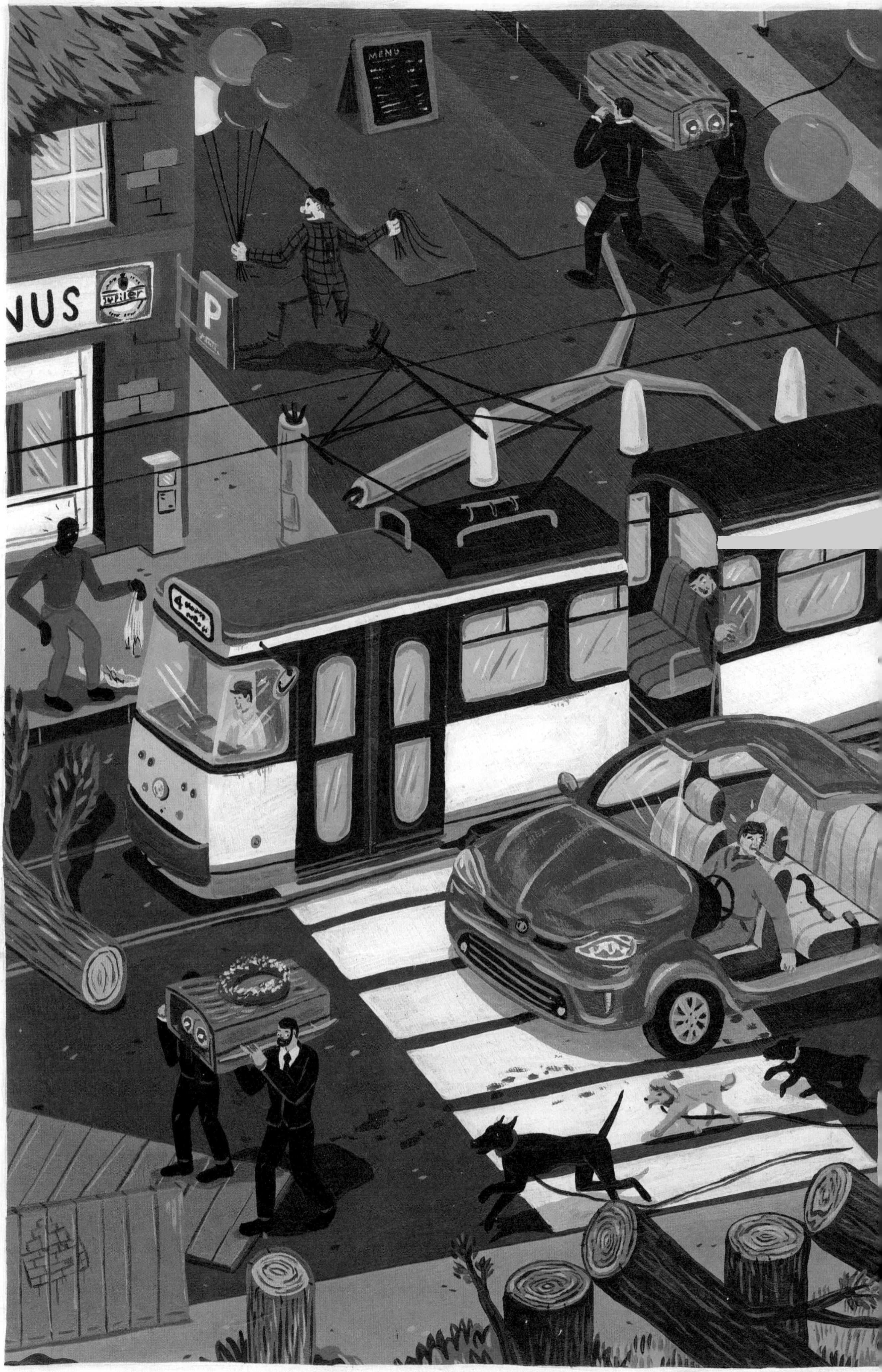
MENU
NUS
P
4

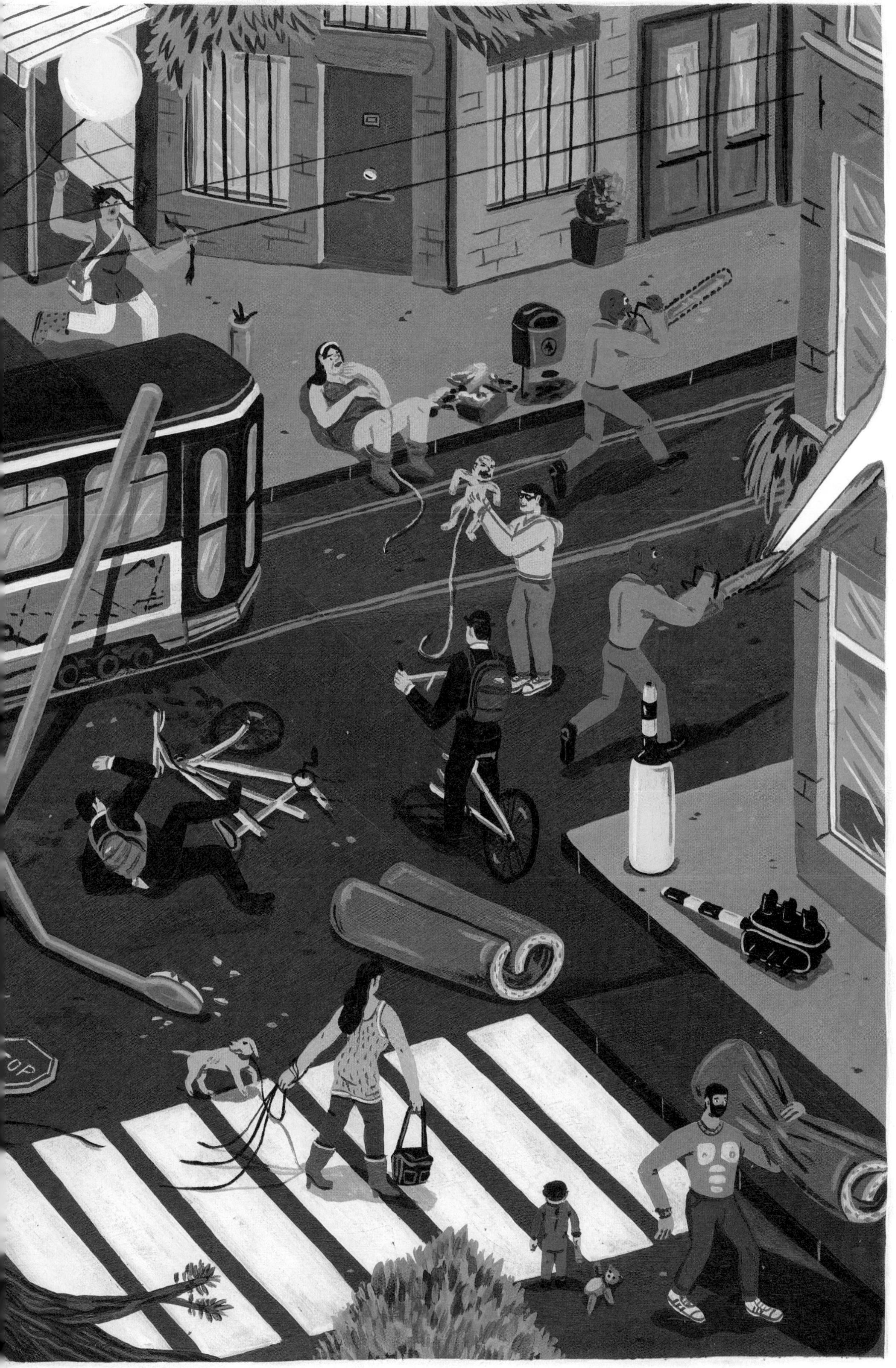

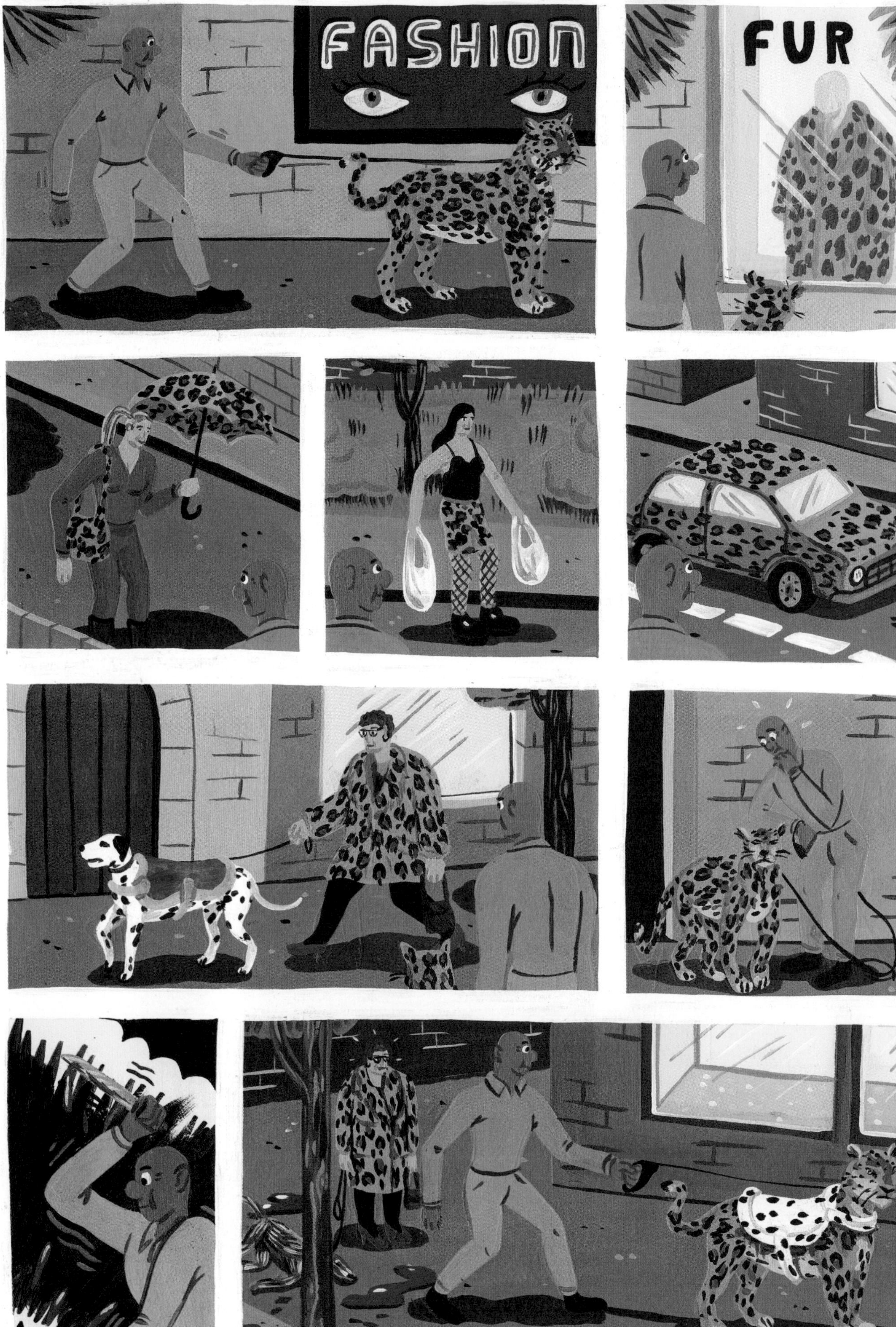
FASHION
FUR

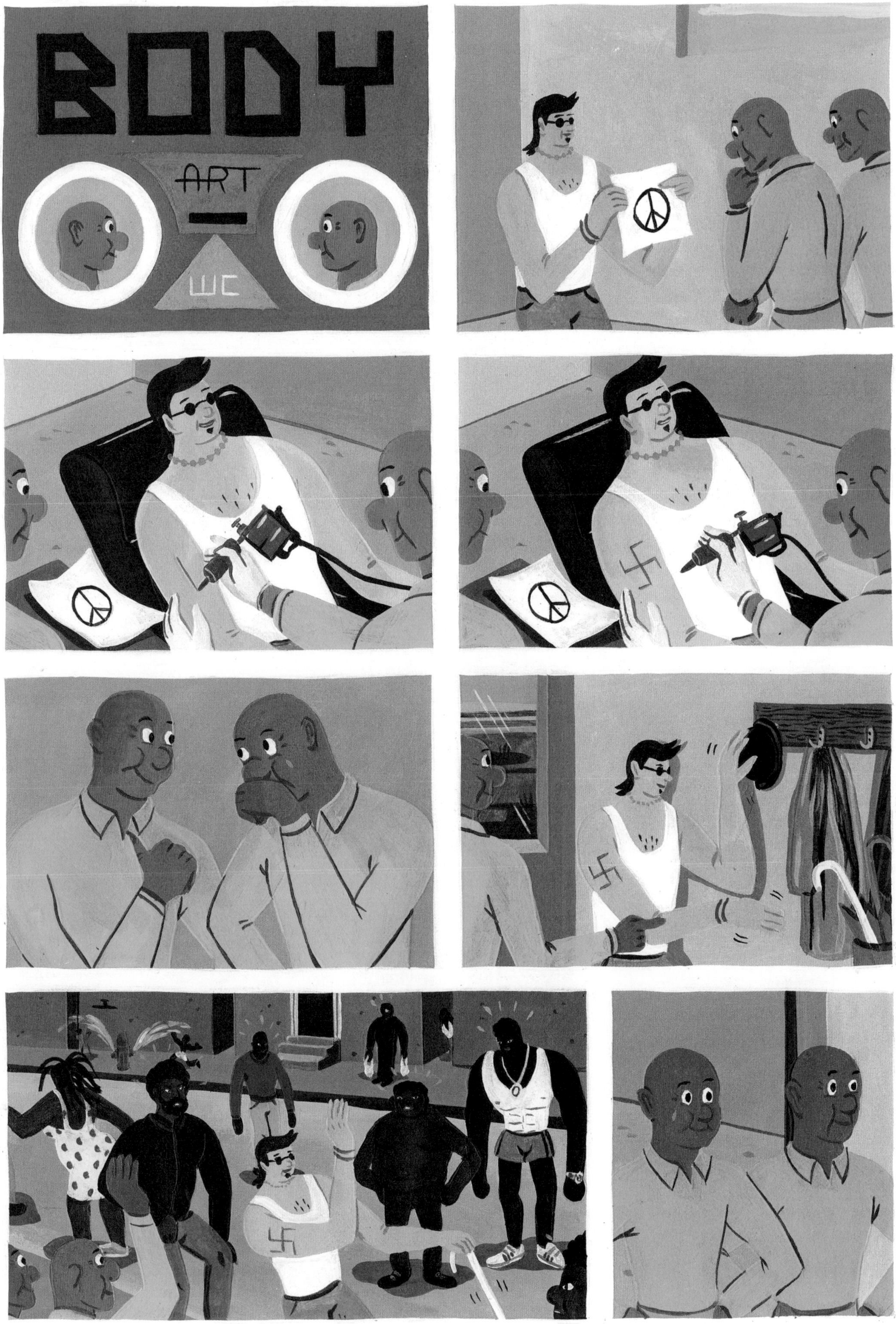
BODY
ART
WC

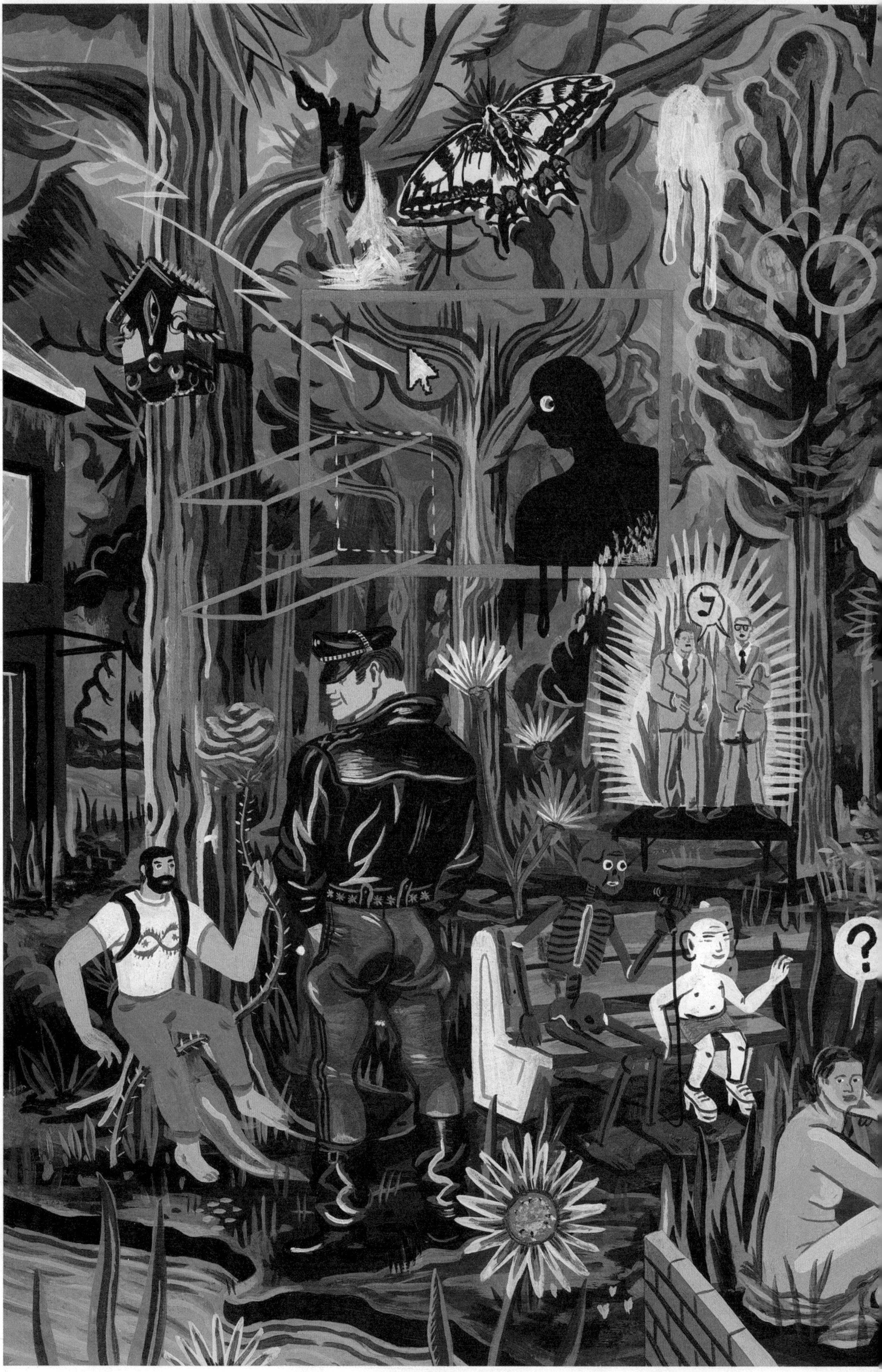
?

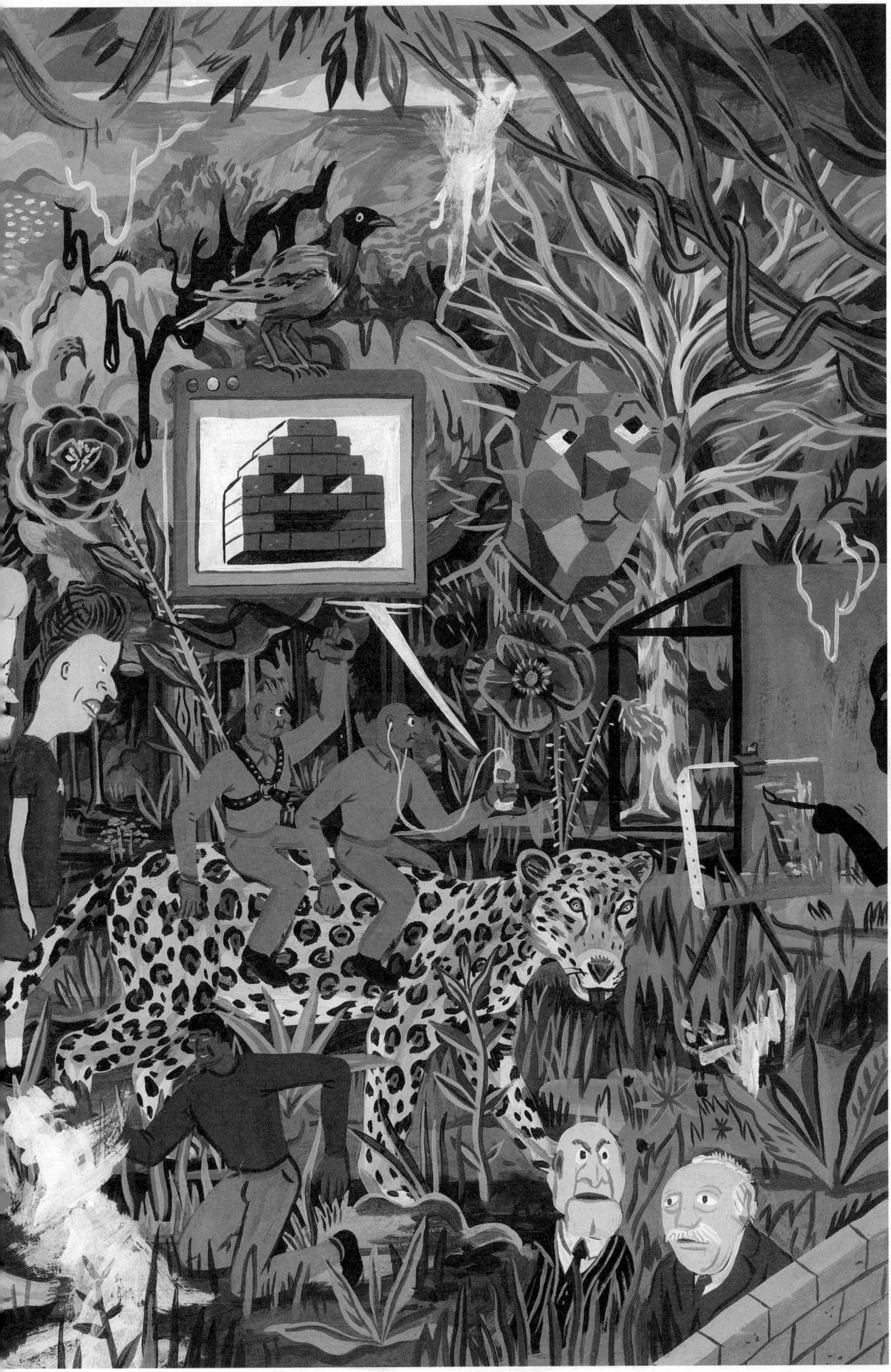

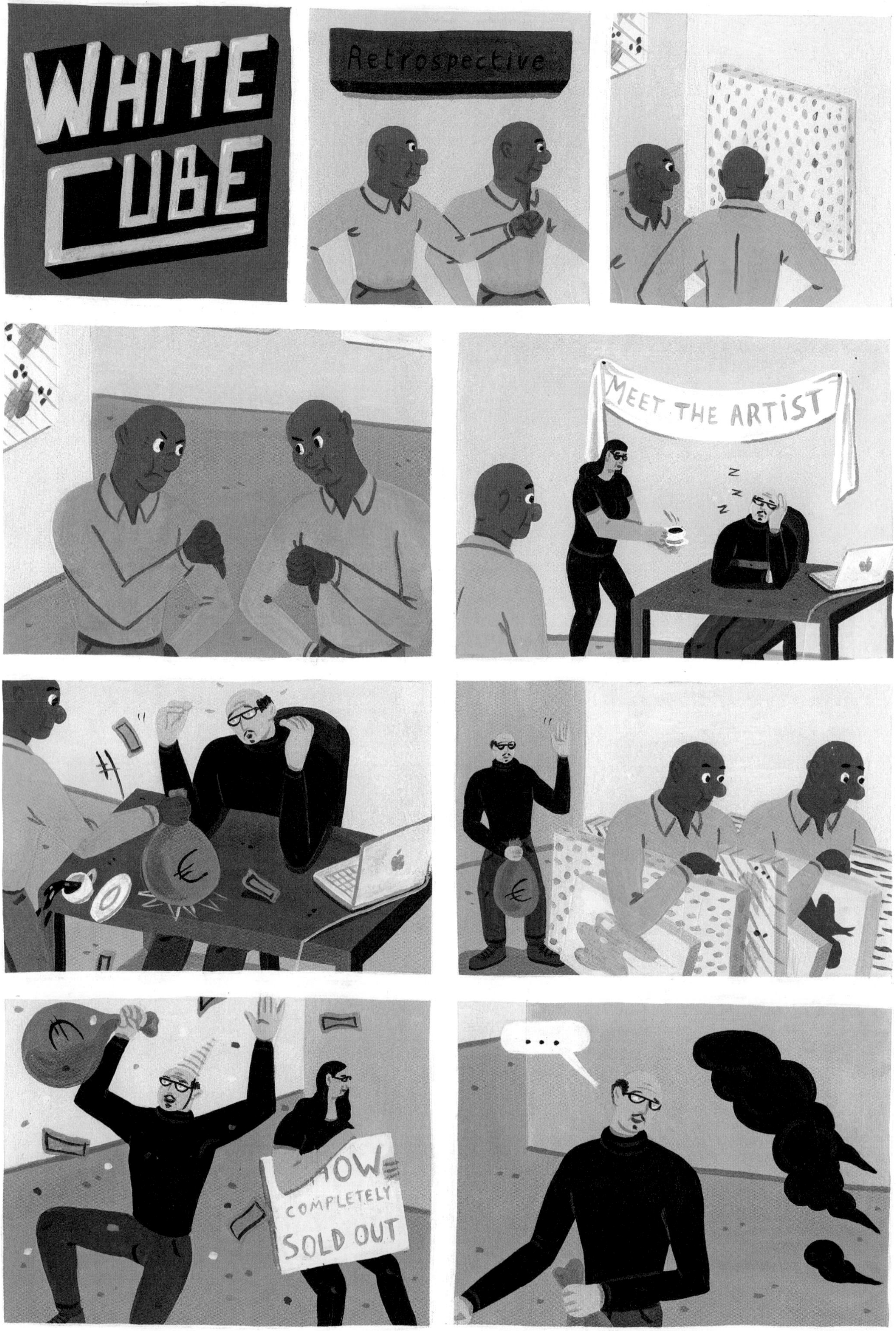
WHITE CUBE
Retrospective
MEET THE ARTIST
Z Z Z
SHOW COMPLETELY SOLD OUT
...

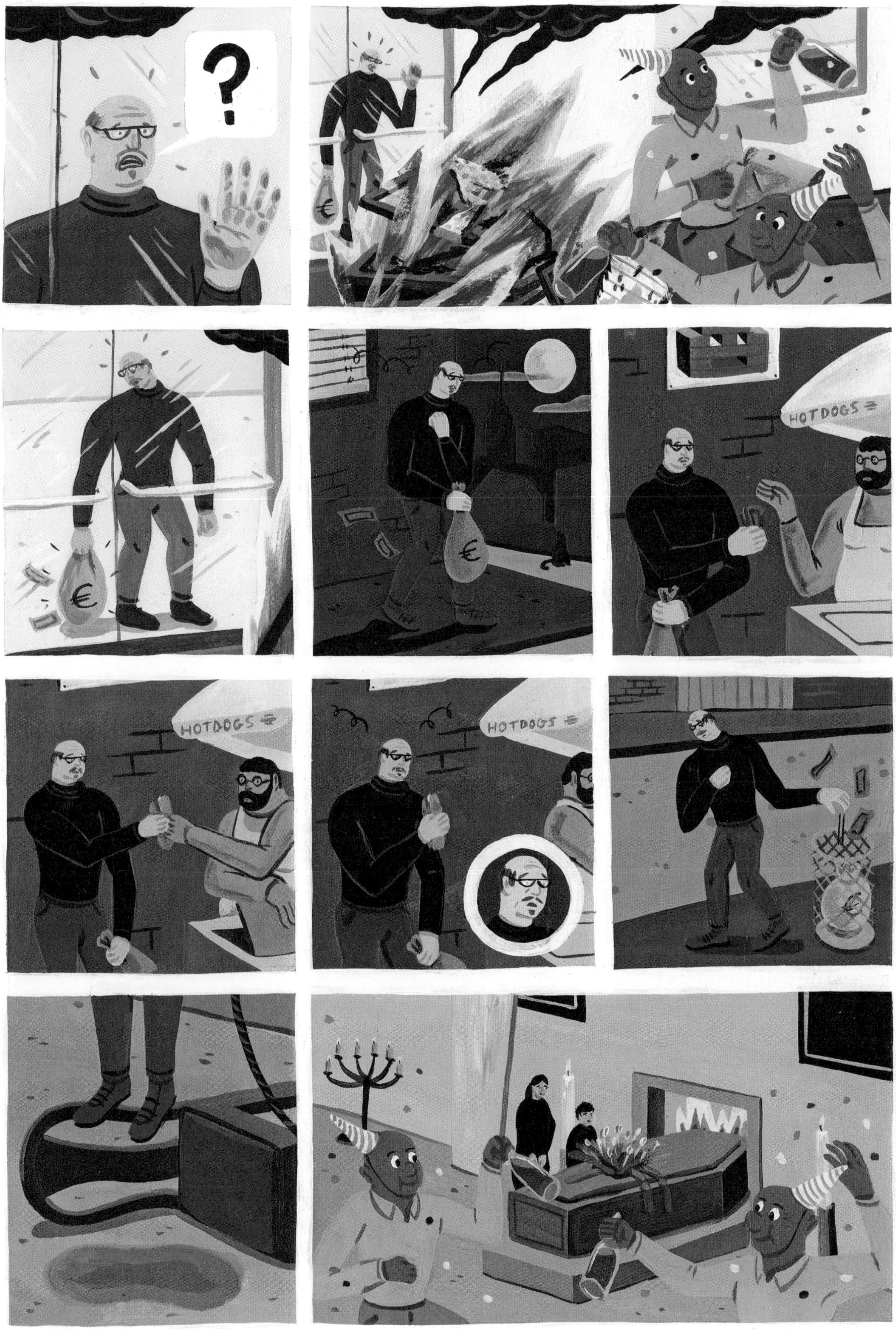
?
HOTDOGS
HOTDOGS
HOTDOGS

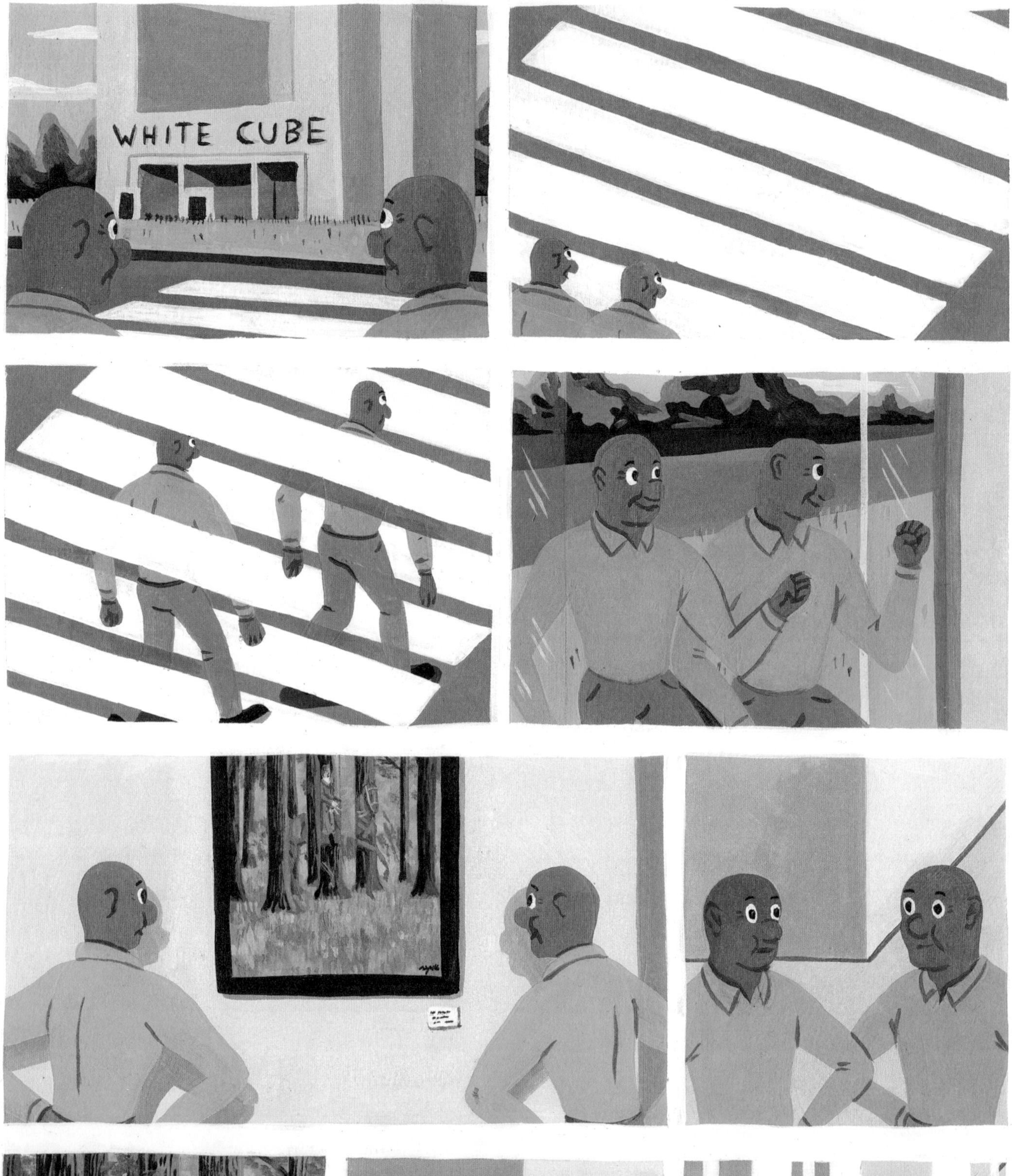
WHITE CUBE

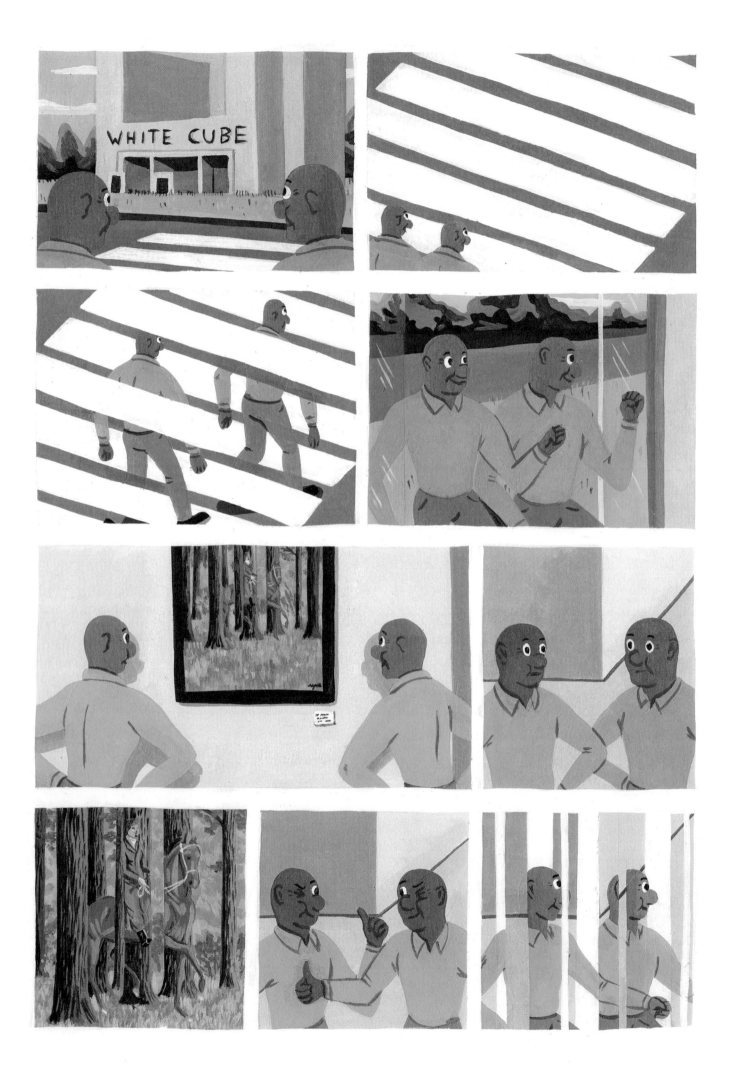

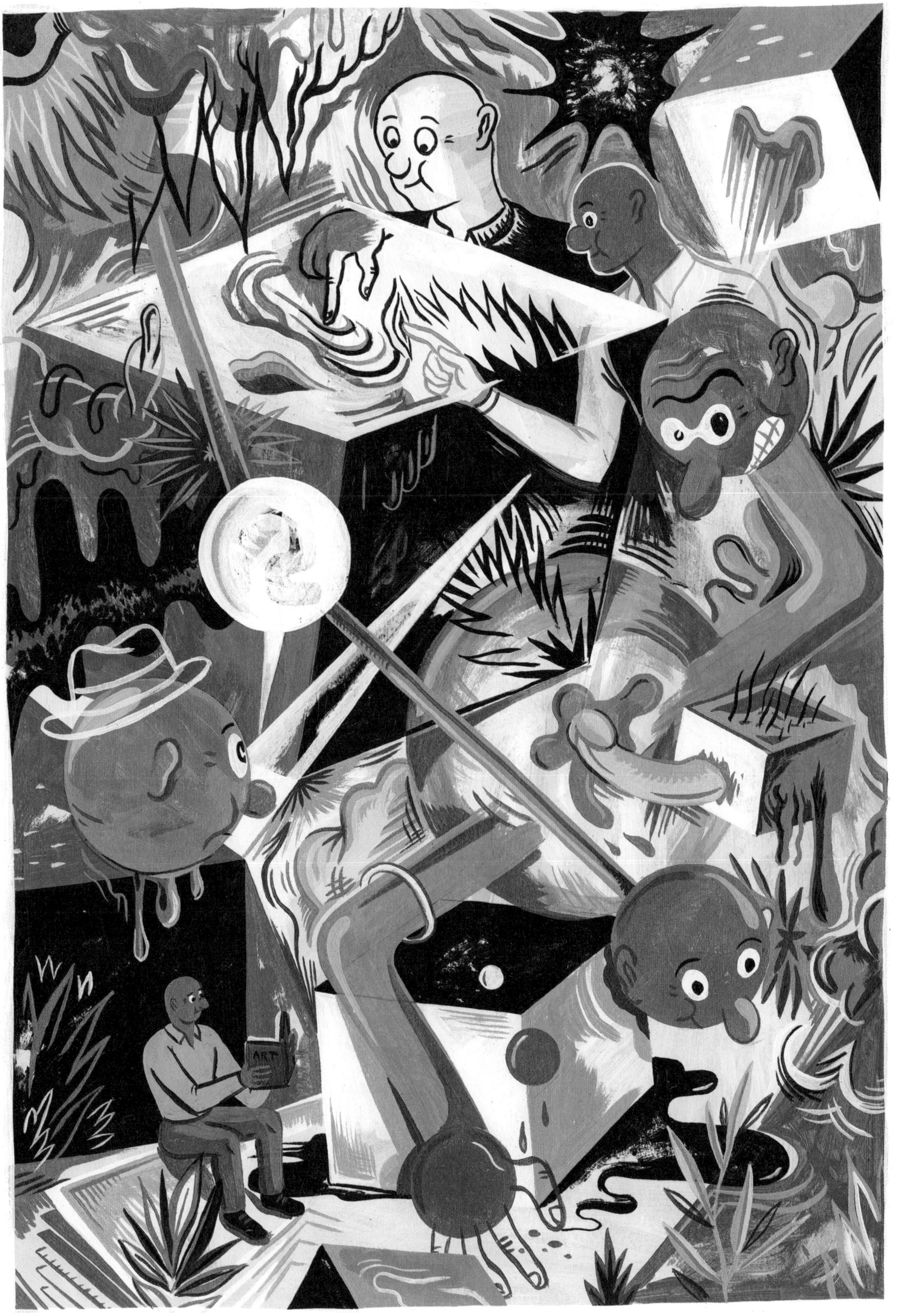
ART

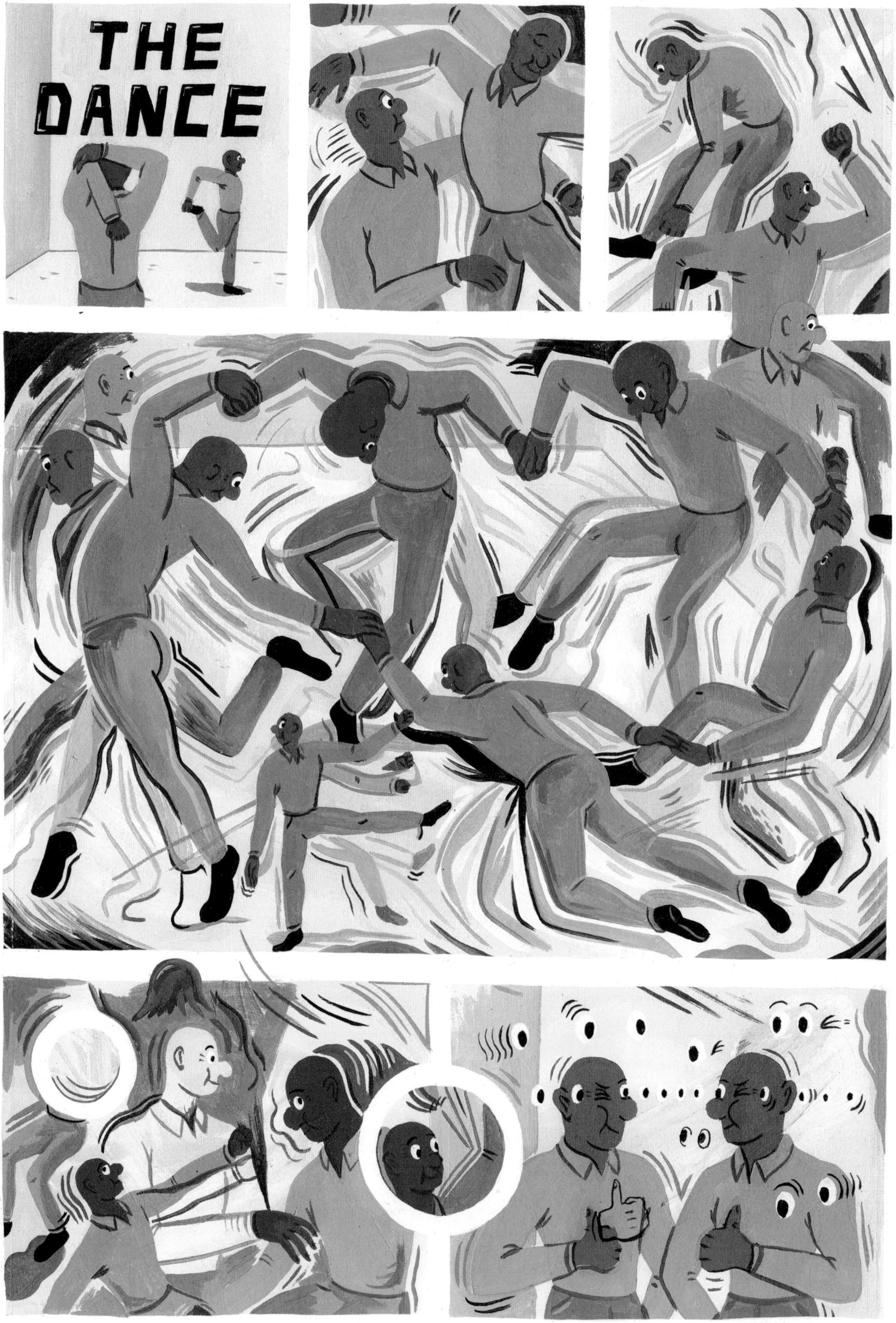
THE DANCE

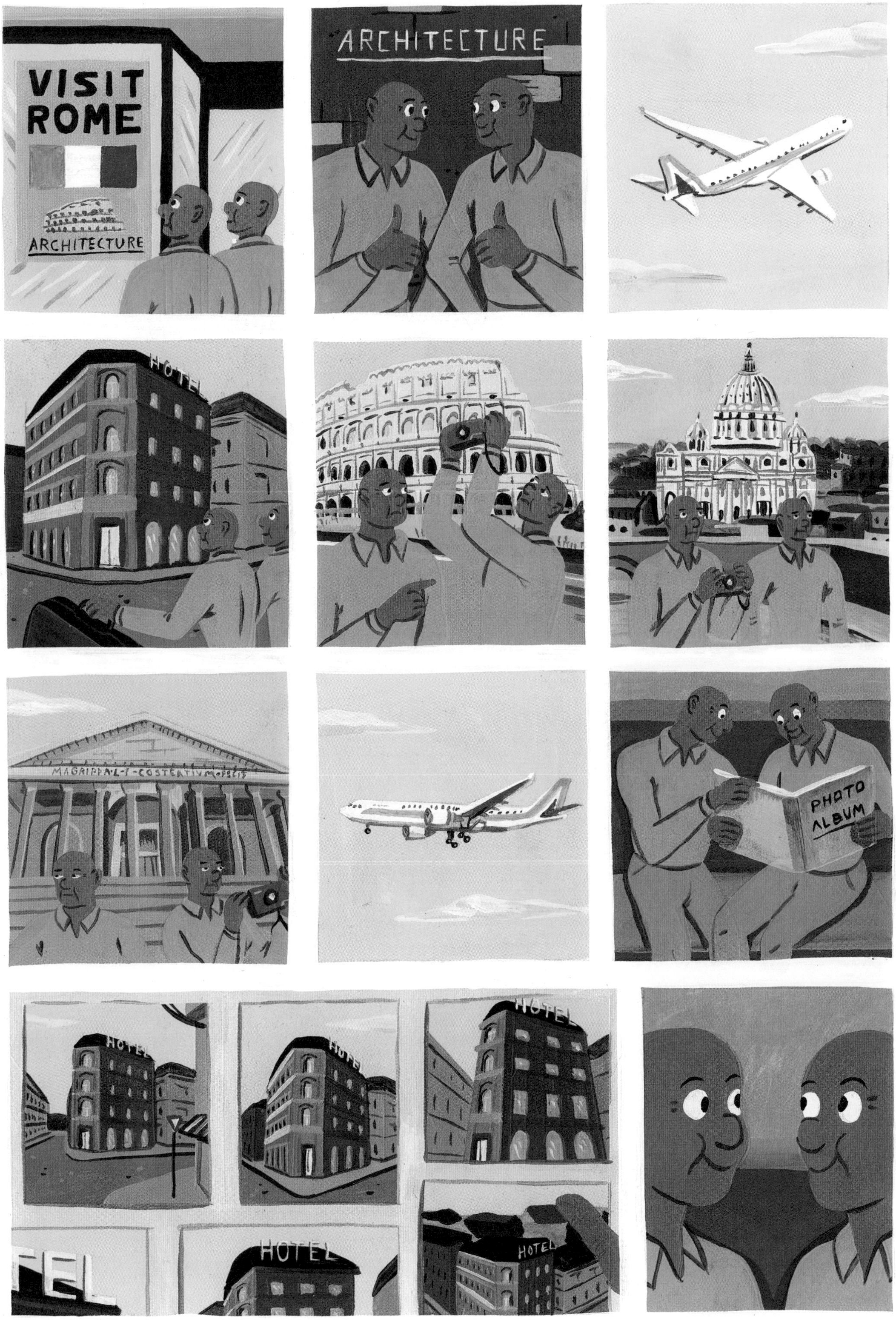
VISIT ROME
ARCHITECTURE
ARCHITECTURE
HOTEL
PHOTO ALBUM
HOTEL
HOTEL
HOTEL
HOTEL
HOTEL

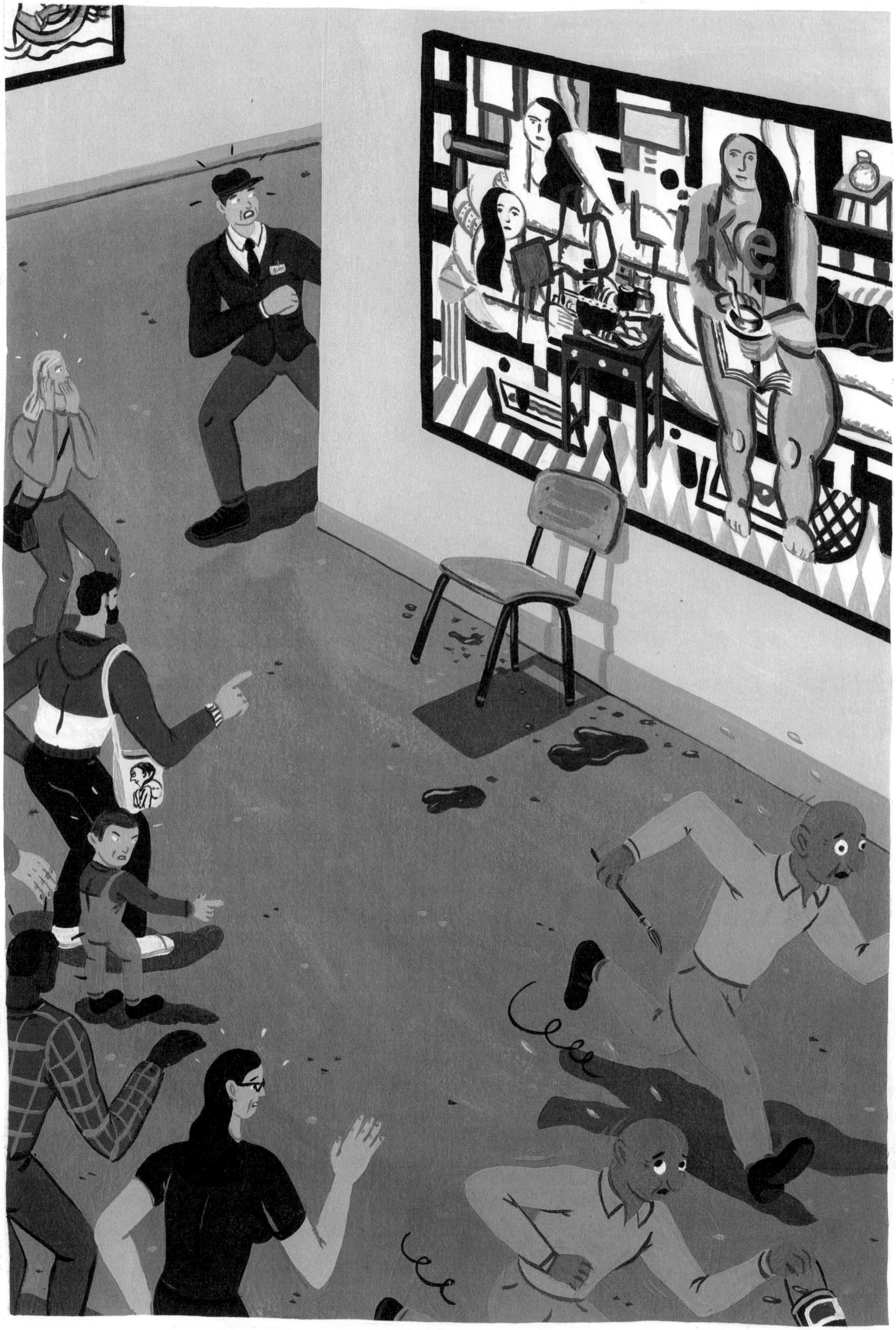
Like

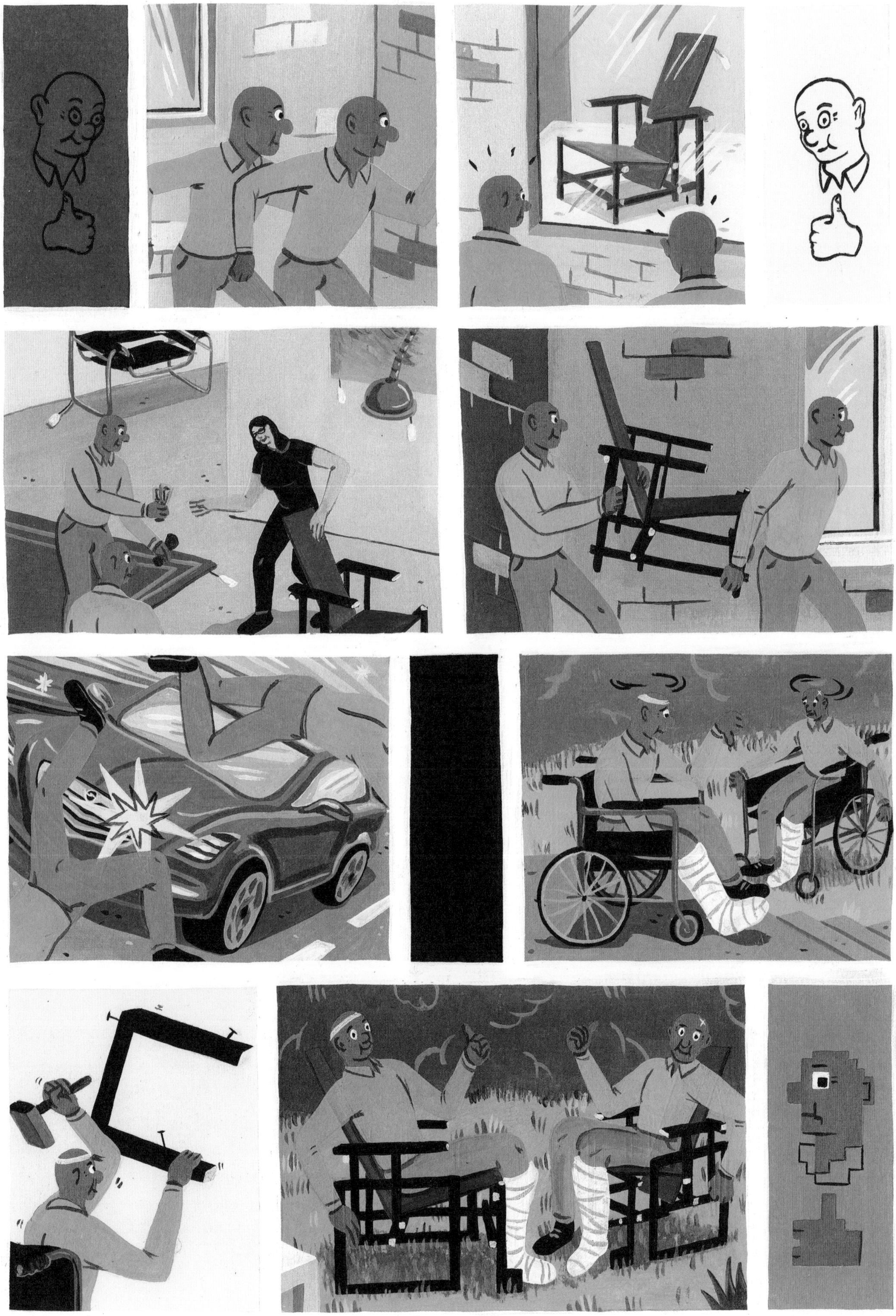

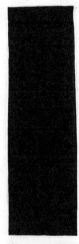

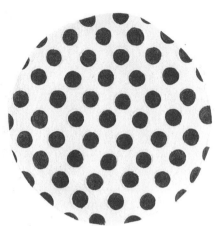

M-MAYBE HE BECAME ILL AND COULDN'T LEAVE THE STUDIO!

MUSEUM BAR

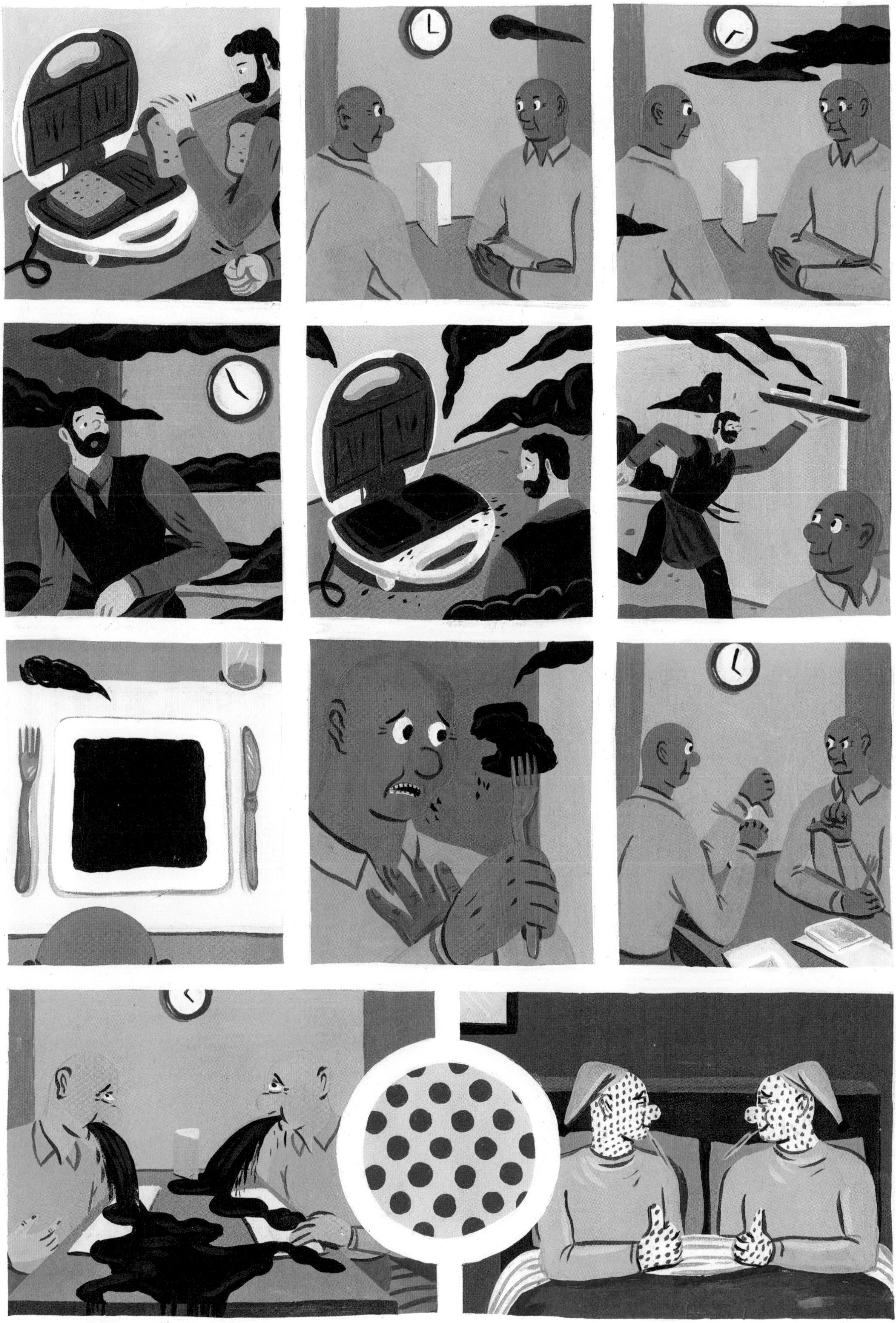

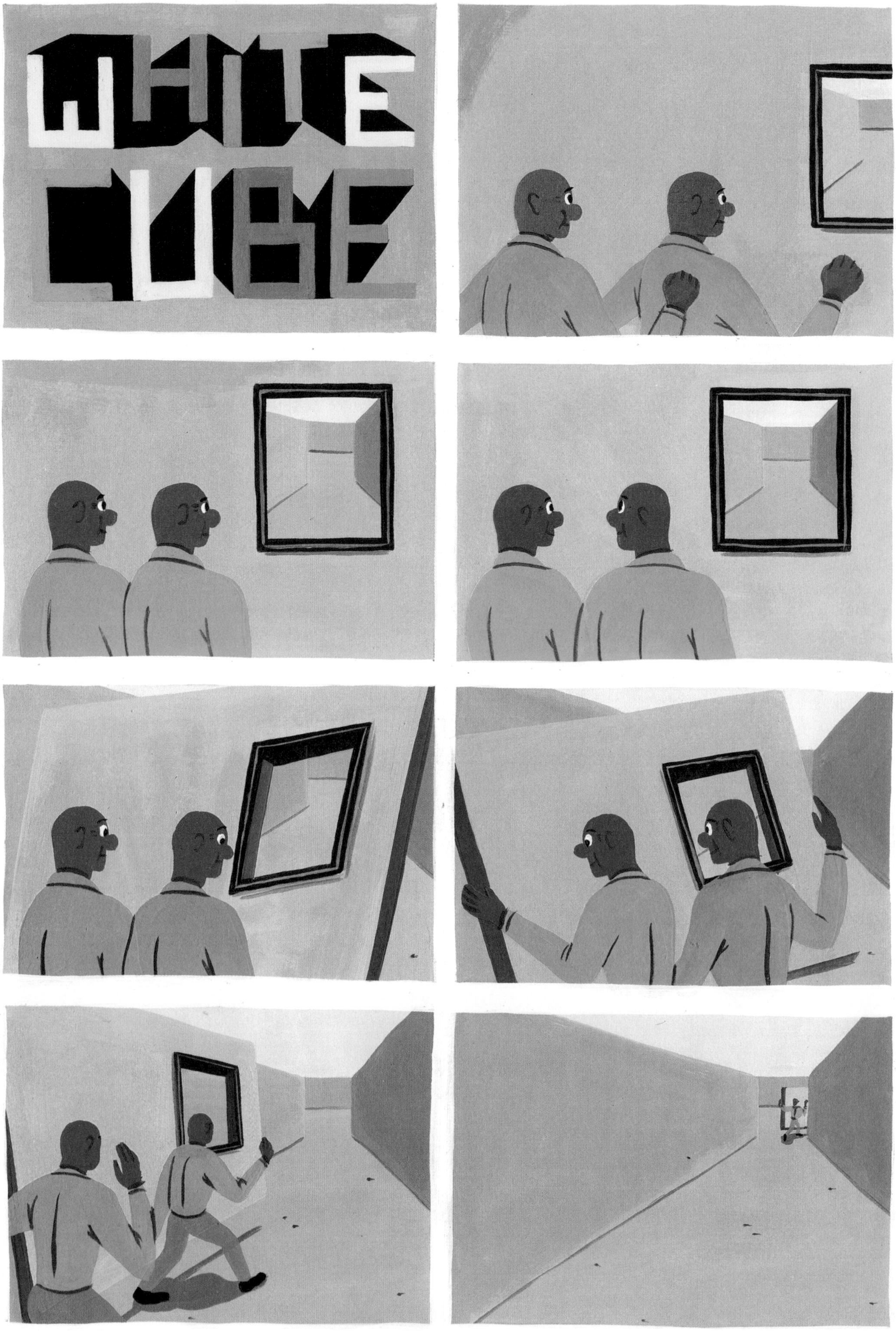
WHITE
CUBE

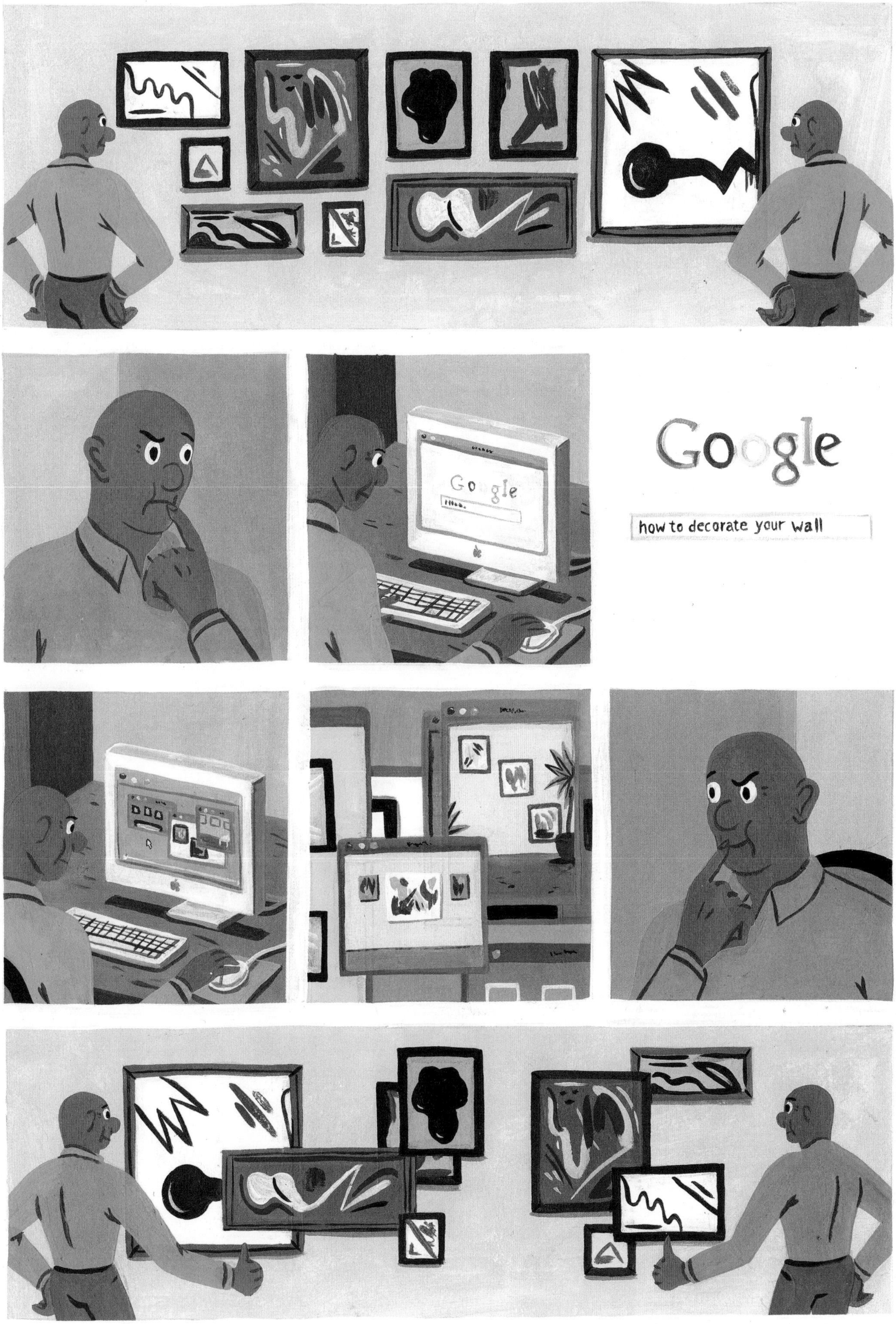
Google
how to decorate your wall

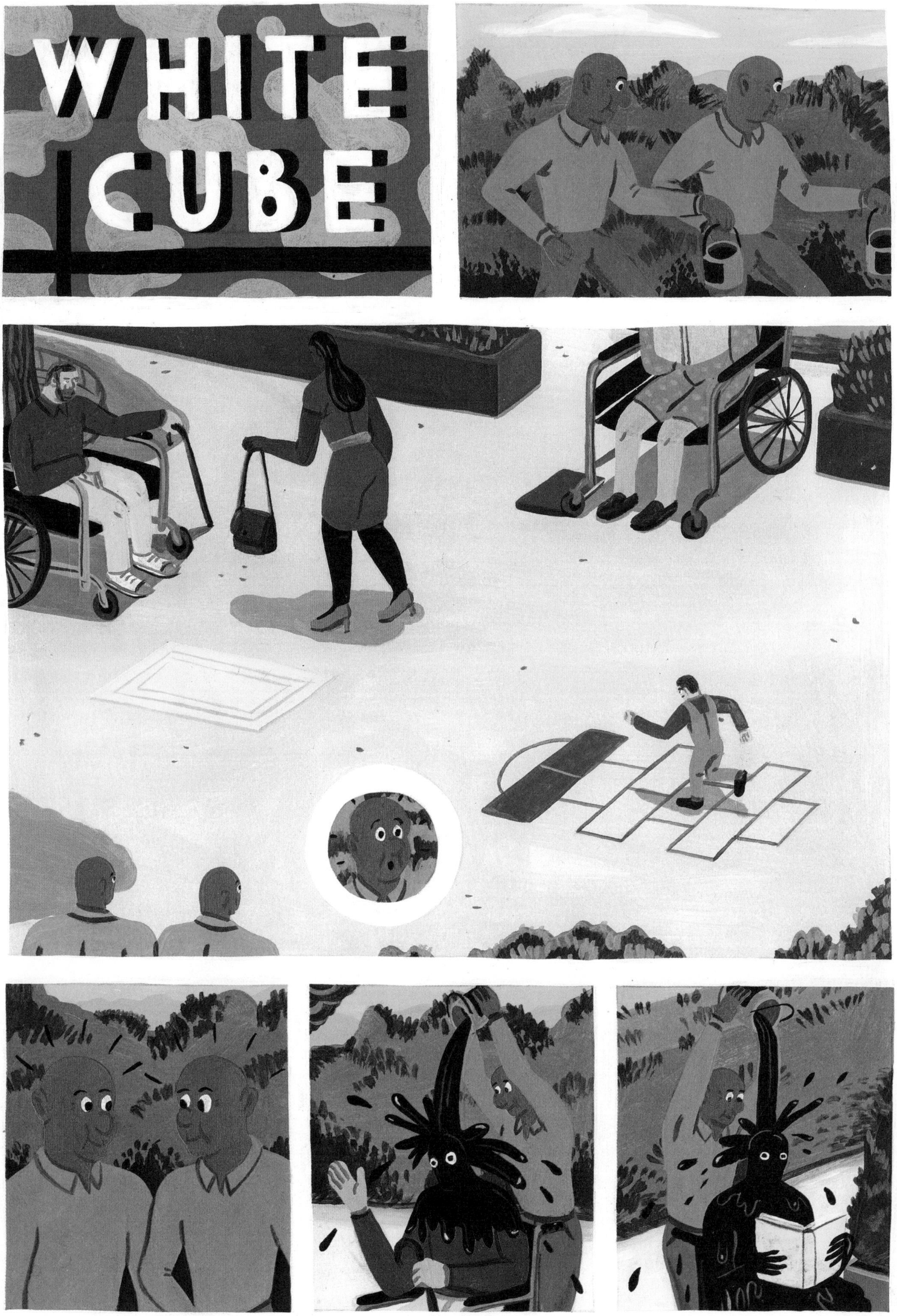
WHITE
CUBE

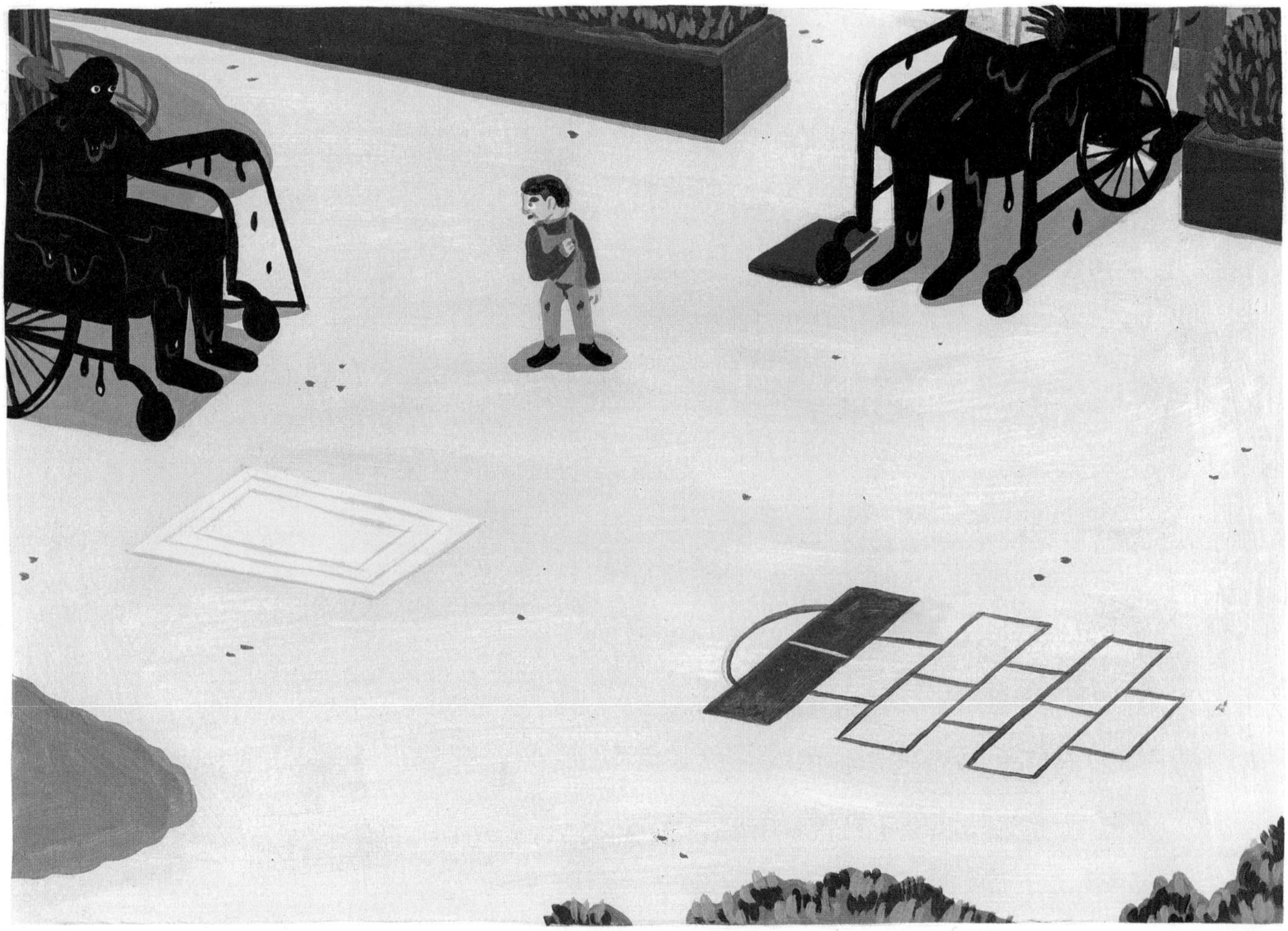

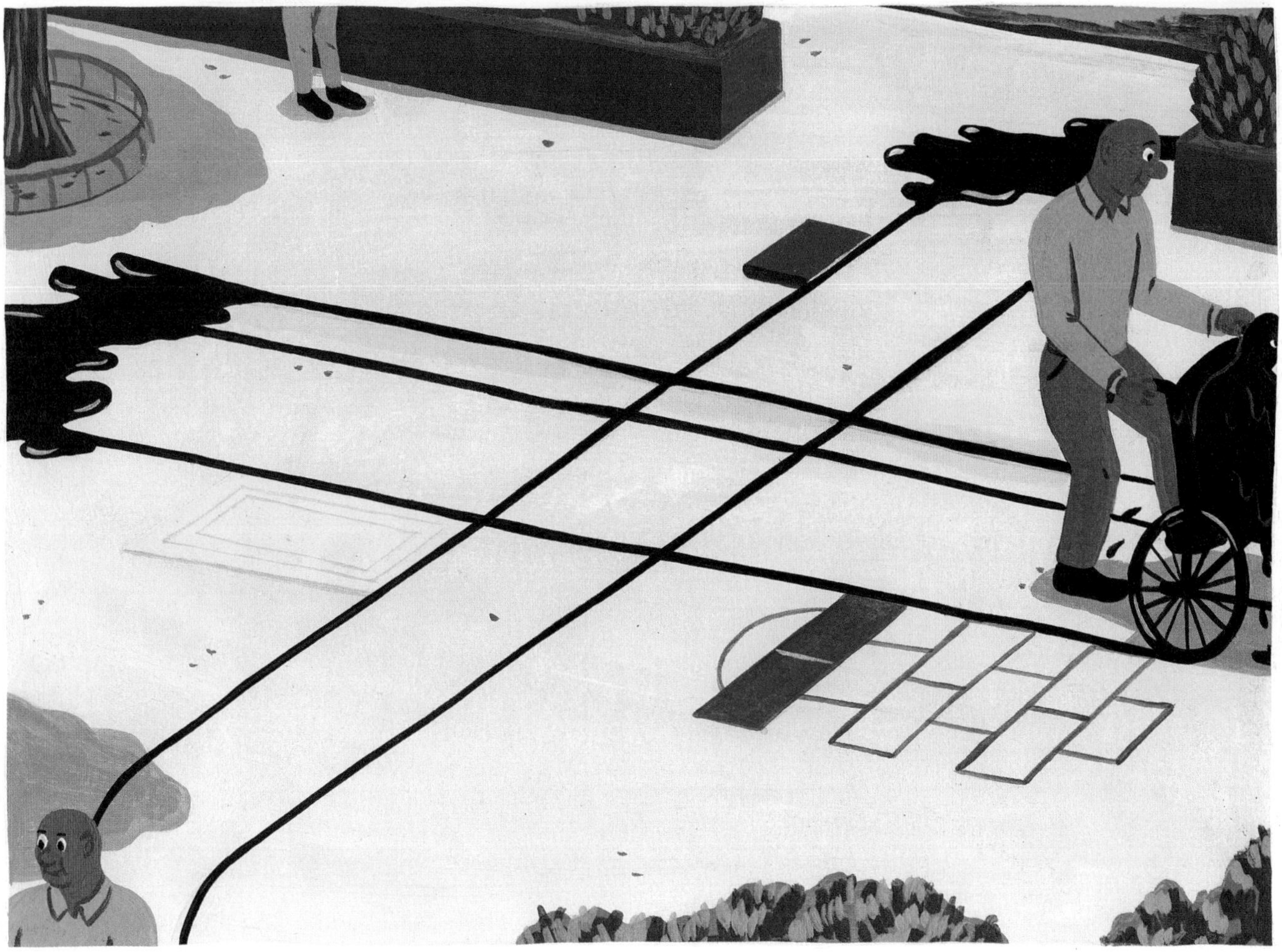

WHITE CUBE
the artist is present...

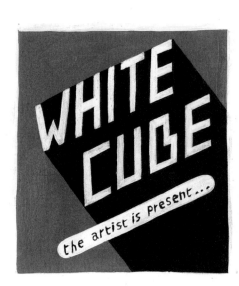

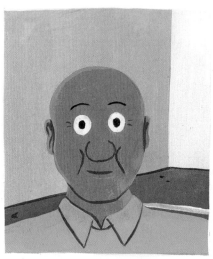

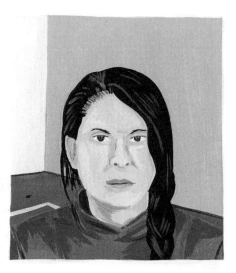

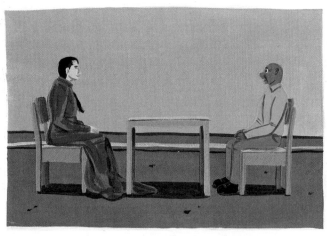

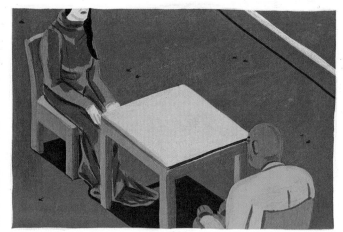

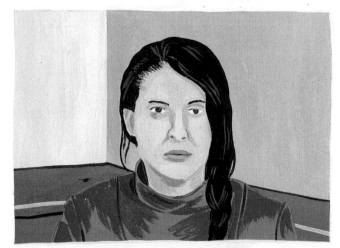

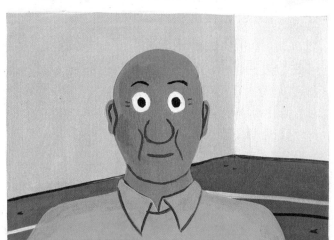

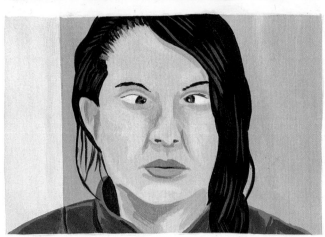

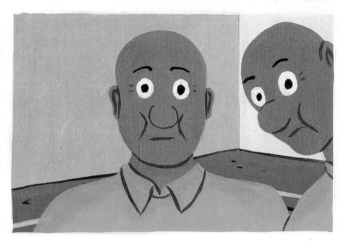

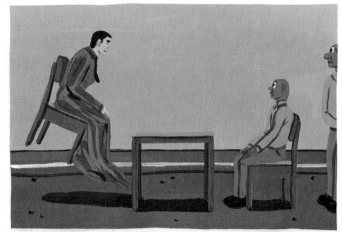
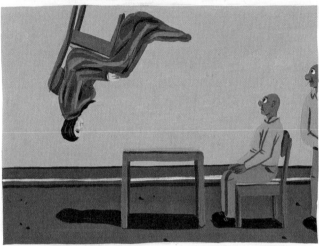

ABRAMOVIĆ

VISITOR

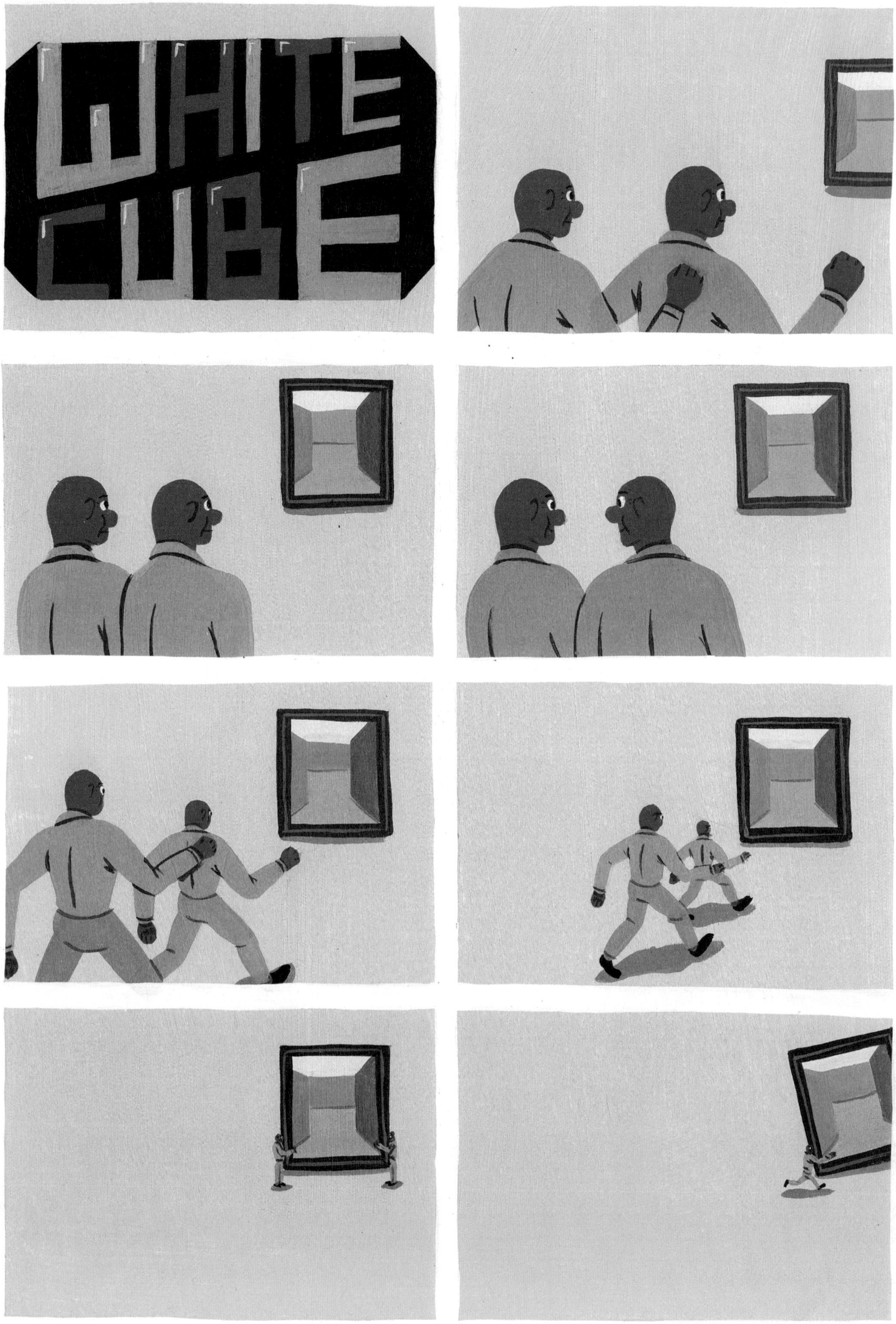
WHITE
CUBE

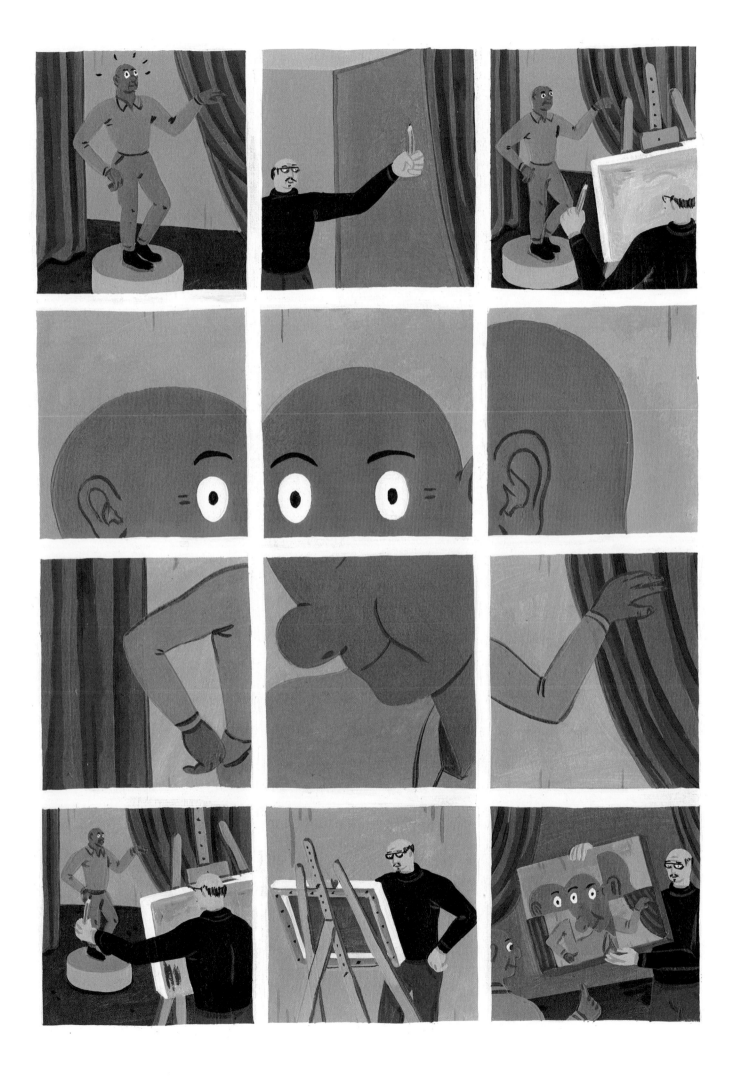

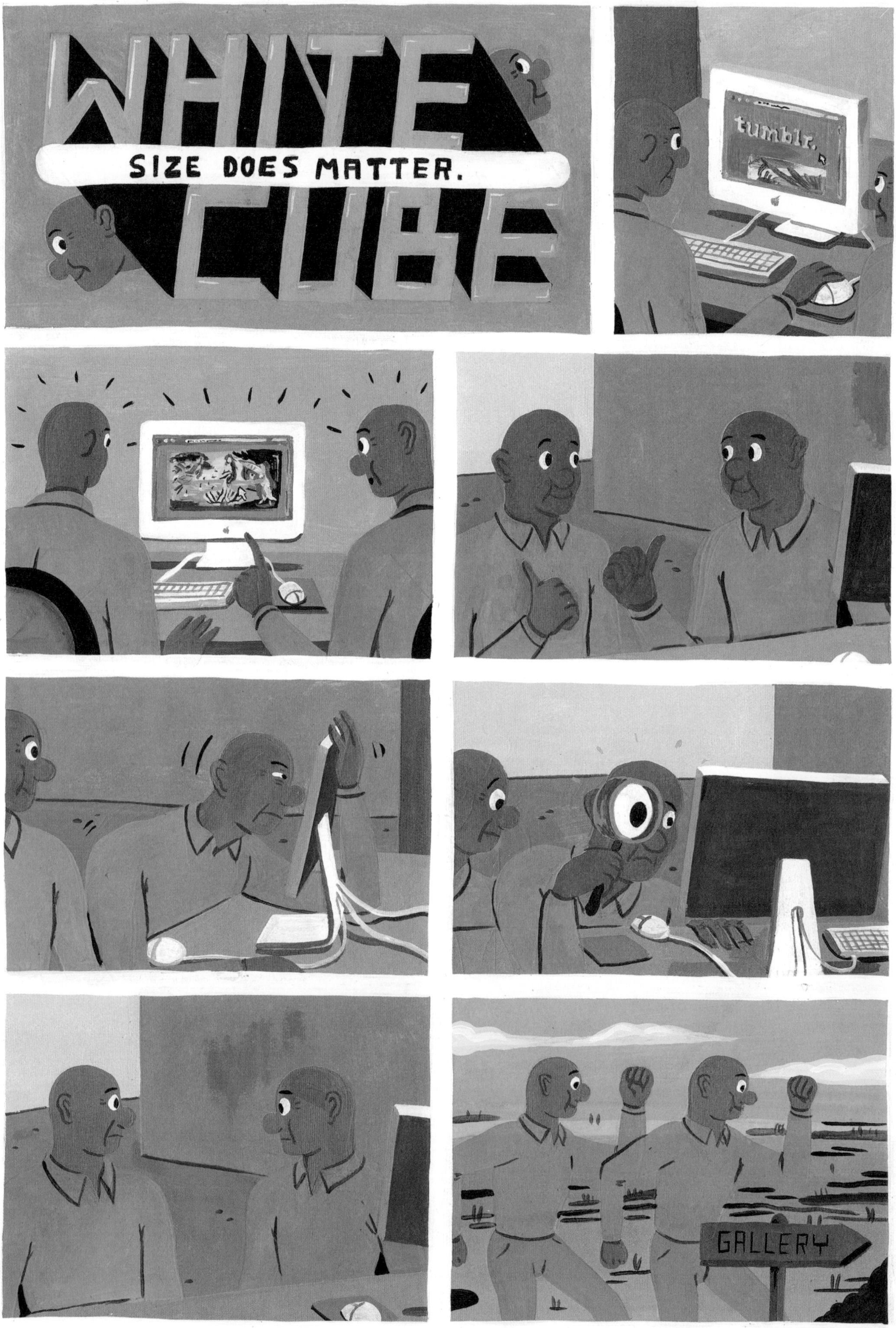
WHITE CUBE
SIZE DOES MATTER.
tumblr.
GALLERY

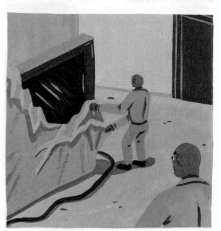

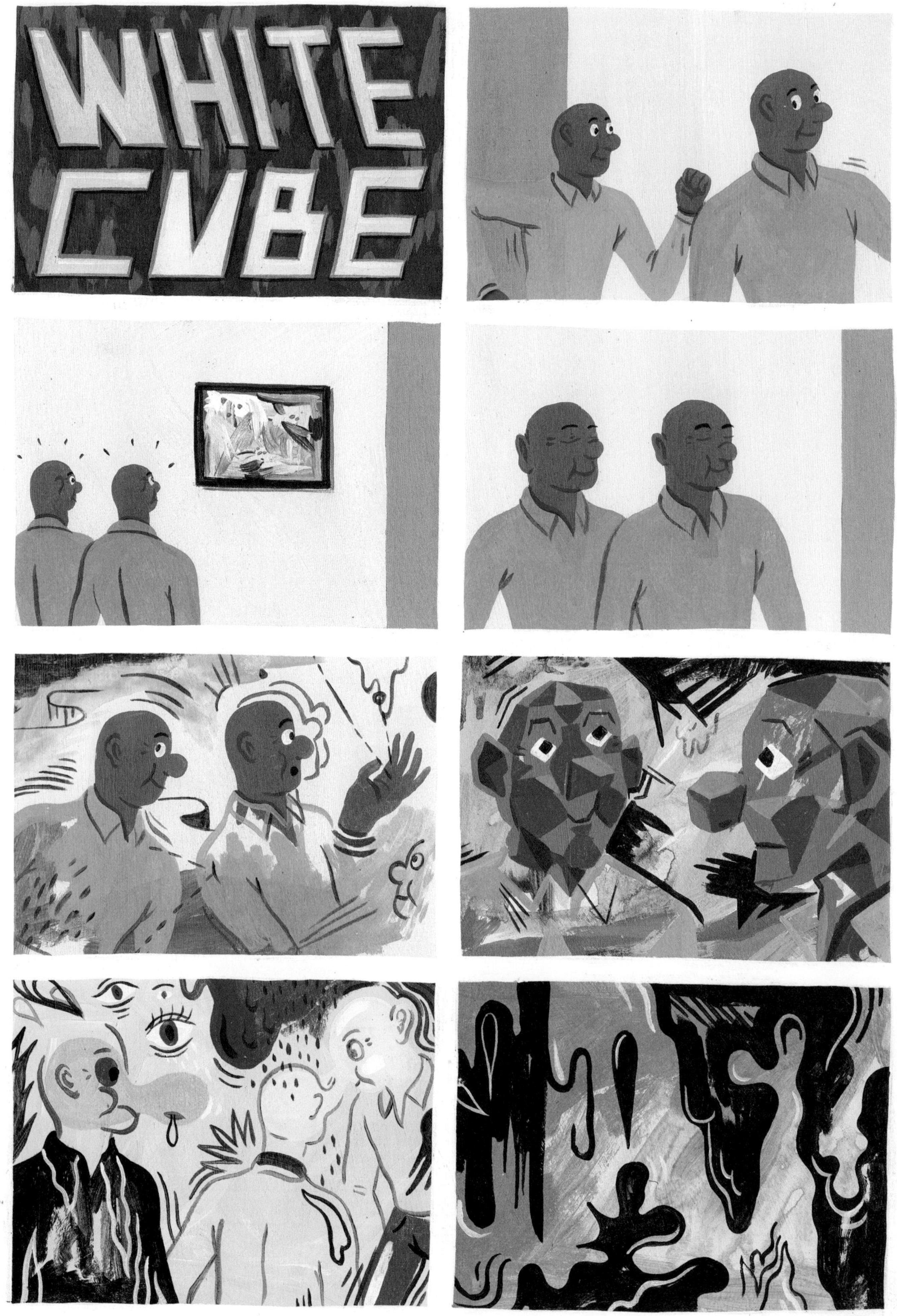
WHITE
CVBE

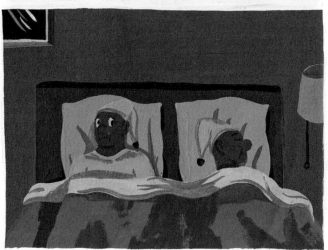

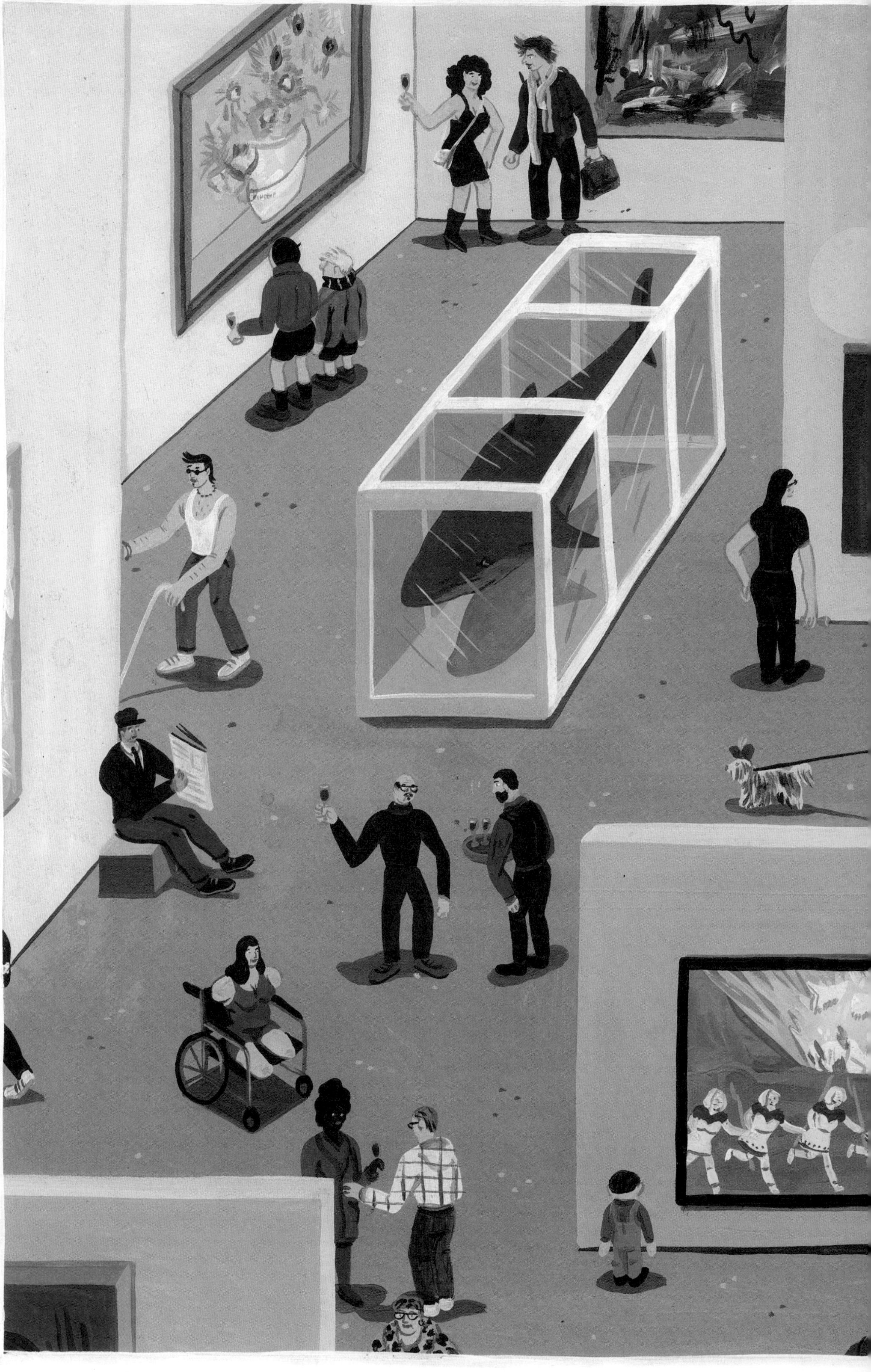

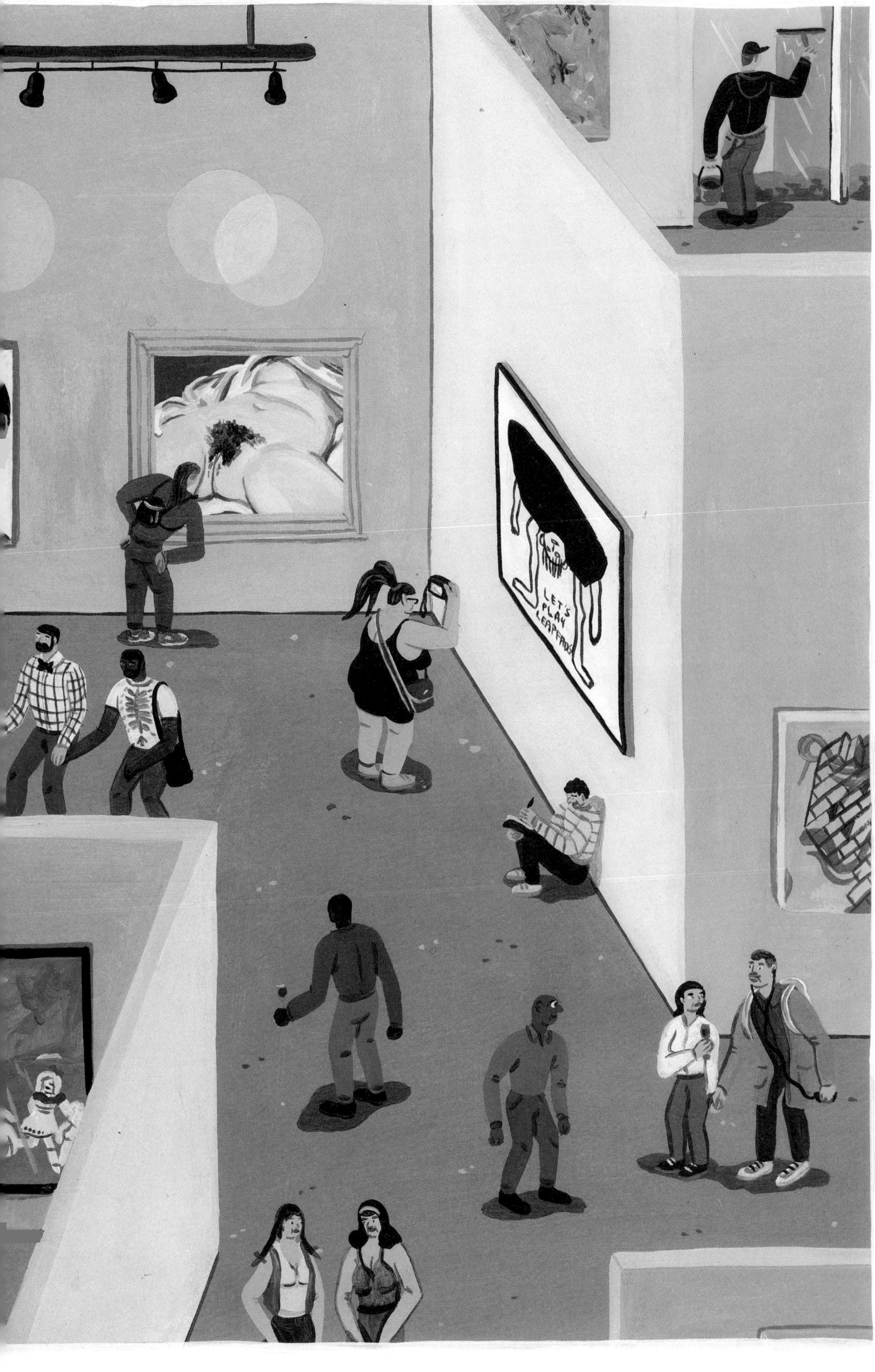
LET'S PLAY LEAPFROG

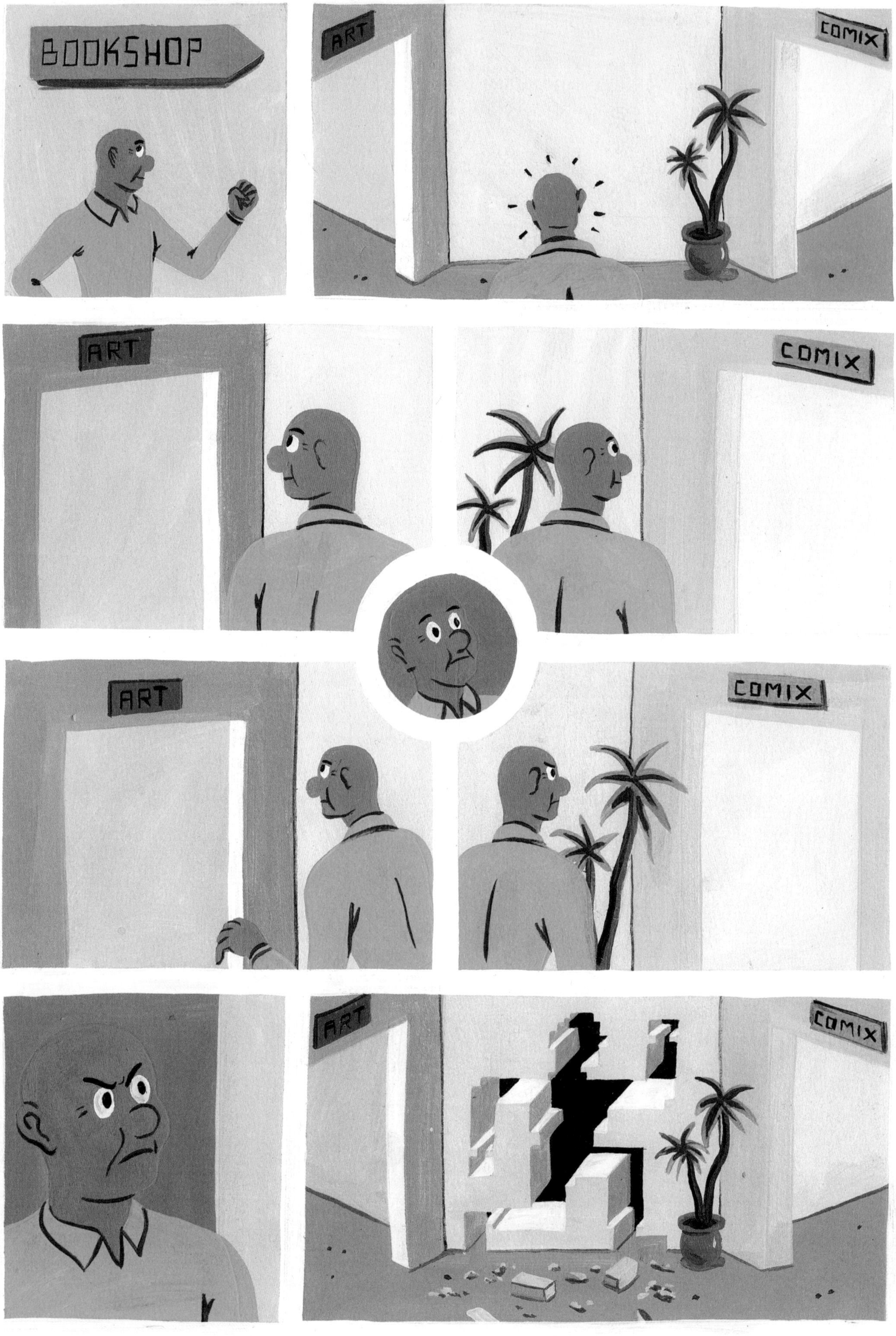
BOOKSHOP
ART
COMIX
ART
COMIX
ART
COMIX
ART
COMIX